Philip Roth

The Facts

In 1997 Philip Roth won the Pulitzer Prize for *American Pastoral*. In 1998 he received the National Medal of Arts at the White House and in 2002 the highest award of the American Academy of Arts and Letters, the Gold Medal in Fiction. He twice won the National Book Award and the National Book Critics Circle Award. He won the PEN/ Faulkner Award three times. In 2005 *The Plot Against America* received the Society of American Historians' Prize for "the outstanding historical novel on an American theme for 2003–2004." Roth received PEN's two most prestigious awards: in 2006 the PEN/Nabokov Award and in 2007 the PEN/Bellow Award for achievement in American fiction. In 2011 he received the National Humanities Medal at the White House and was later named the fourth recipient of the Man Booker International Prize. He died in 2018.

VINTAGE

INTERNATIONAL

BOOKS BY PHILIP ROTH

ZUCKERMAN BOOKS
The Ghost Writer
Zuckerman Unbound
The Anatomy Lesson
The Prague Orgy

The Counterlife

American Pastoral
I Married a Communist
The Human Stain

Exit Ghost

ROTH BOOKS
The Facts · Deception
Patrimony · Operation Shylock
The Plot Against America

KEPESH BOOKS
The Breast
The Professor of Desire
The Dying Animal

NEMESES: SHORT NOVELS
Everyman · Indignation
The Humbling · Nemesis

MISCELLANY
Reading Myself and Others
Shop Talk

OTHER BOOKS
Goodbye, Columbus · Letting Go
When She Was Good · Portnoy's Complaint · Our Gang
The Great American Novel · My Life as a Man
Sabbath's Theater

The Facts

Philip Roth

The Facts

A NOVELIST'S AUTOBIOGRAPHY

Vintage International

VINTAGE BOOKS

A DIVISION OF PENGUIN RANDOM HOUSE LLC

NEW YORK

FIRST VINTAGE INTERNATIONAL EDITION, FEBRUARY 1997

Sections of this book first appeared, in slightly different form, in the
Atlantic, The New York Times Book Review, and *Vanity Fair.*

Library of Congress Cataloging-in-Publication Data
Roth, Philip.
The facts : a novelist's autobiography / by Philip Roth.—1st Vintage International ed.
p.   cm.
1. Roth, Philip—Biography. 2. Novelists, American—20th century—Biography.
I. Title.
PS3568.O855Z467   1997
813'.54   96-28807
[B]—DC20
CIP

Vintage International Trade Paperback ISBN: 978-0-679-74905-9

www.vintagebooks.com

To my brother at sixty

And as he spoke I was thinking, *the kind of stories that people turn life into, the kind of lives that people turn stories into.*

Nathan Zuckerman, in *The Counterlife*

The Facts

Dear Zuckerman,

In the past, as you know, the facts have always been note-book jottings, my way of springing into fiction. For me, as for most novelists, every genuine imaginative event begins down there, with the facts, with the specific, and not with the philo-sophical, the ideological, or the abstract. Yet, to my surprise, I now appear to have gone about writing a book absolutely backward, taking what I have already imagined and, as it were, desiccating it, so as to restore my experience to the original, prefictionalized factuality. Why? To prove that there is a sig-nificant gap between the autobiographical writer that I am thought to be and the autobiographical writer that I am? To prove that the information that I drew from my life was, in the fiction, incomplete? If that was all, I don't think I would have gone to the trouble, since thoughtful readers, if they were interested enough to care, could have figured as much for themselves. Nor was there any call for this book; no one ordered it, no one sent down for an autobiography from Roth. The order, if it was ever even placed, went out thirty years ago, when certain of my Jewish elders demanded to know just who this kid was who was writing this stuff.

No, the thing seems to have been born out of other necessities, and sending this manuscript to you—and asking you, as I do, to tell me whether you think I should publish it— prompts me to explain what may have led to my presenting myself in prose like this, undisguised. Until now I have always used the past as the basis for transformation, for, among other things, a kind of intricate explanation to myself of my world. Why appear untransformed in front of people when, by and large, in the unimagined world, I've refrained from nakedly divulging my personal life to (and pressing a TV personality on) a serious audience? On the pendulum of self-exposure that oscillates between aggressively exhibitionistic Mailerism and sequestered Salingerism, I'd say that I occupy a midway position, trying in the public arena to resist gratuitous prying or preening without making too holy a fetish of secrecy and seclusion. So why claim biographical visibility now, especially as I was educated to believe that the independent reality of the fiction is all there is of importance and that writers should remain in the shadows?

Well, to begin to answer—the person I've intended to make myself visible to here has been myself, primarily. Over fifty you need ways of making yourself visible to yourself. A moment comes, as it did for me some months back, when I was all at once in a state of helpless confusion and could not understand any longer what once was obvious to me: why I do what I do, why I live where I live, why I share my life with the one I do. My desk had become a frightening, foreign place and, unlike similar moments earlier in life when the old strategies didn't work anymore—either for the pragmatic business of daily living, those problems that everybody faces, or for the specialized problems of writing—and I had energetically resolved on a course of renewal, I came to believe that I just could not make myself over yet again. Far from feeling capable of remaking myself, I felt myself coming undone.

I'm talking about a breakdown. Although there's no need to delve into particulars here, I will tell you that in the spring of 1987, at the height of a ten-year period of creativity, what was to have been minor surgery turned into a prolonged physical ordeal that led to an extreme depression that carried me right to the edge of emotional and mental dissolution. It was in the period of post-crack-up meditation, with the clarity attending the remission of an illness, that I began, quite involuntarily, to focus virtually all my waking attention on worlds from which I had lived at a distance for decades—remembering where I had started out from and how it had all begun. If you lose something, you say, "Okay, let's retrace the steps. I came in the house, took off my coat, went into the kitchen," etc., etc. In order to recover what I had lost I had to go back to the moment of origin. I found no one moment of origin but a series of moments, a history of multiple origins, and that's what I have written here in the effort to repossess life. I hadn't ever mapped out my life like this but rather, as I've said, had looked only for what could be transformed. Here, so as to fall back into my former life, to retrieve my vitality, to transform myself into *myself*, I began rendering experience untransformed.

Perhaps it wasn't even myself I wanted to be turned into but the boy I had been when I went off to college, the boy surrounded on the playground by his neighborhood compatriots—back down to ground zero. After the crack-up comes the grateful rush into ordinary life, and that was my life at its most ordinary. I suppose I wanted to return to the point when the launch was the launch of a more ordinary Roth and, at the same time, to reengage those formative encounters, to reclaim the earliest struggles, to get back to that high-spirited moment when the manic side of my imagination took off and I became my own writer; back to the original well, not for material but for the launch, the *re*launch—out of fuel, back to tank up on the magic blood. Like you, Zuckerman, who are reborn in *The Counterlife* through your English wife, like your brother, Henry, who seeks rebirth in Israel with his West Bank fundamentalists, just as both of you in the same book miraculously manage to be revived from death, I too was ripe for another chance. If while writing I couldn't see exactly what I was up to, I do now: this manuscript embodies *my* counterlife, the antidote and answer to all those fictions that culminated in the fiction of you. If in one way *The Counterlife* can be read as fiction about structure, then this is the bare bones, the structure of a life without the fiction.

As a matter of fact, the two longish works of fiction about you, written over a decade, were probably what made me sick of fictionalizing myself further, worn out with coaxing into existence a being whose experience was comparable to my own and yet registered a more powerful valence, a life more highly charged and energized, more entertaining than my own . . . which happens to have been largely spent, quite unentertainingly, alone in a room with a typewriter. I was depleted by the rules I'd set myself—by having to imagine things not quite as they had happened to me or things that never happened to me or things that couldn't possibly have happened to me happening to an agent, a projection of mine, to a kind of me. If this manuscript conveys anything, it's my exhaustion with masks, disguises, distortions, and lies.

Of course, even without the crack-up and the need for self-investigation it generated, I might have found myself, at this moment, unable to wield the whip over the facts sufficiently to make real life amazing. Undermining experience, embellishing experience, rearranging and enlarging experience into a species of mythology—after thirty years at that, it could have seemed like I'd had enough even under the best of circumstances. To demythologize myself and play it straight, to pair the facts as lived with the facts as presented might well have seemed the next thing to do—if not the only thing I *could* do—so long as the capacity for self-transformation and, with it, the imagination were at the point of collapse. Insofar as the rest of me, which had collapsed as well, intuited that stripping the writing down to unvarnished specificity was a part of getting back what I'd lost, a means of recovery and a way to strength, there wasn't even a choice. I needed clarification, as much of it as I could get—demythologizing to induce depathologizing.

This isn't to say that I didn't have to resist the impulse to dramatize untruthfully the insufficiently dramatic, to complicate the essentially simple, to charge with implication what implied very little—the temptation to abandon the facts when those facts were not so compelling as others I might imagine if I could somehow steel myself to overcome fiction-fatigue. But on the whole it was easier than I thought it would be to escape from what I'd felt constrained to do nearly every day of the pre-crack-up existence. Perhaps that's because in its uncompelling, unferocious way, the nonfictional approach has brought me closer to how experience actually *felt* than has turning the flame up under my life and smelting stories out of all I've known. I'm not arguing that there's a kind of existence that exists in fiction that doesn't exist in life or vice versa but simply saying that a book that faithfully conforms to the facts, a distillation of the facts that leaves off with the imag-

inative fury, can unlock meanings that fictionalizing has ob-
scured, distended, or even inverted and can drive home some
sharp emotional nails.

I recognize that I'm using the word "facts" here, in this
letter, in its idealized form and in a much more simpleminded
way than it's meant in the title. Obviously the facts are never
just coming at you but are incorporated by an imagination
that is formed by your previous experience. Memories of the
past are not memories of facts but memories of your imag-
inings of the facts. There is something naïve about a novelist
like myself talking about presenting himself "undisguised"
and depicting "a life without the fiction." I also invite over-
simplification of a kind I don't at all like by announcing that
searching out the facts may have been a kind of therapy for
me. You search your past with certain questions on your
mind—indeed, you search out your past to discover which
events have led you to asking those specific questions. It isn't
that you subordinate your ideas to the force of the facts in
autobiography but that you construct a sequence of stories to
bind up the facts with a persuasive *hypothesis* that unravels
your history's meaning. I suppose that calling this book *The
Facts* begs so many questions that I could manage to be both
less ironic and more ironic by calling it *Begging the Question*.

A final observation about the predicament that engendered
The Facts, and then you may read on undisturbed. Though
I can't be entirely sure, I wonder if this book was written not
only out of exhaustion with making fictional self-legends and
not only as a spontaneous therapeutic response to my crack-
up but also as a palliative for the loss of a mother who still,
in my mind, seems to have died inexplicably—at seventy-
seven in 1981—as well as to hearten me as I come closer and
closer and closer to an eighty-six-year-old father viewing the
end of life as a thing as near to his face as the mirror he shaves

in (except that this mirror is there day and night, directly in front of him all the time). Even though it might not be apparent to others, I think that subterraneanly my mother's death is very strong in all this, as is observing my provident father preparing for no future, a healthy but very old man dealing with the kind of feelings aroused by an incurable illness, because just like those who are incurably ill, the aged know everything about their dying except exactly when.

I wonder if a breakdown-induced eruption of parental longing in a fifty-five-year-old man isn't, in fact, the Rosetta stone to this manuscript. I wonder if there hasn't been some consolation, particularly while recovering my equilibrium, in remembering that when the events narrated here were happening we all were there, nobody having gone away or been on the brink of going away, never to be seen again for hundreds of thousands of billions of years. I wonder if I haven't drawn considerable consolation from reassigning myself as myself to a point in life when the grief that may issue from the death of parents needn't be contended with, when it is unperceivable and unsuspected, and one's own departure is unconceivable because they are there like a blockade.

I think that's everything that might lie behind this book. The question now is, why should anybody other than me be reading it, especially as I acknowledge that they've gotten a good bit of it elsewhere, under other auspices? Especially as I consider myself, partly through this effort, united again with my purposes and reengaged with life. Especially as this feels like the first thing that I have ever written *unconsciously* and sounds to me more like the voice of a twenty-five-year-old than that of the author of my books about you. Especially as publication would leave me feeling exposed in a way I don't particularly wish to be exposed.

There's also the problem of exposing others. While writing,

when I began to feel increasingly squeamish about confessing intimate affairs of mine to *everybody*, I went back and changed the real names of some of those with whom I'd been involved, as well as a few identifying details. This was not because I believed that the rerendering would furnish complete anonymity (it couldn't make those people anonymous to their friends and mine) but because it might afford at least a little protection from their being pawed over by perfect strangers.

Beyond these considerations that make publication problematic for me stands *the* question: Is the book any good? Because *The Facts* has meant more to me than may be obvious and because I've never worked before without my imagination having been fired by someone like you or Portnoy or Tarnopol or Kepesh, I'm in no real position to tell.

Be candid.

Sincerely,

Roth

Prologue

One day in late October 1944, I was astonished to find my
father, whose workday ordinarily began at seven and many
nights didn't end until ten, sitting alone at the kitchen table
in the middle of the afternoon. He was going into the hospital
unexpectedly to have his appendix removed. Though he had
already packed a bag to take with him, he had waited for my
brother, Sandy, and me to get home from school to tell us
not to be alarmed. "Nothing to it," he assured us, though we
all knew that two of his brothers had died back in the 1920s
from complications following difficult appendectomies. My
mother, the president that year of our school's parent-teacher
association, happened, quite unusually, to be away overnight
in Atlantic City at a statewide PTA convention. My father had
phoned her hotel, however, to tell her the news, and she had
immediately begun preparations to return home. That would

do it, I was sure: my mother's domestic ingenuity was on a par with Robinson Crusoe's, and as for nursing us all through our illnesses, we couldn't have received much better care from Florence Nightingale. As was usual in our household, everything was now under control.

By the time her train pulled into Newark that evening, the surgeon had opened him up, seen the mess, and despaired for my father's chances. At the age of forty-three, he was put on the critical list and given less than a fifty-fifty chance to survive.

Only the adults knew how bad things were. Sandy and I were allowed to go on believing that a father was indestructible—and ours turned out to be just that. Despite a raw emotional nature that makes him prey to intractable worry, his life has been distinguished by the power of resurgence. I've never intimately known anyone else—aside from my brother and me—to swing as swiftly through so wide a range of moods, anyone else to take things so hard, to be so openly racked by a serious setback, and yet, after the blow has reverberated down to the quick, to clamber back so aggressively, to recover lost ground and get going again.

He was saved by the new sulfa powder, developed during the early years of the war to treat battlefront wounds. Surviving was an awful ordeal nonetheless, his weakness from the near-fatal peritonitis exacerbated by a ten-day siege of hiccups during which he was unable to sleep or to keep down food. After he'd lost nearly thirty pounds, his shrunken face disclosed itself to us as a replica of my elderly grandmother's, the face of the mother whom he and all his brothers adored (toward the father—laconic, authoritarian, remote, an immigrant who'd trained in Galicia to be a rabbi but worked in America in a hat factory—their feelings were more confused). Bertha Zahnstecker Roth was a simple old-country woman, good-hearted, given to neither melancholy nor complaint, yet her everyday facial expression made it plain that she nursed no illusions about life's being easy. My father's resemblance to his mother would not appear so eerily again until he himself reached his eighties, and then only when he was in the grip of a struggle that stripped an otherwise physically youthful old man of his seeming impregnability, leaving him bewildered not so much because of the eye problem or the difficulty with his gait that had made serious inroads on his self-sufficiency but because he felt all at once abandoned by that masterful accomplice and overturner of obstacles, his determination.

When he was driven home from Newark's Beth Israel Hospital after six weeks in bed there, he barely had the strength, even with our assistance, to make it up the short back staircase to our second-story apartment. It was December 1944 by then, a cold winter day, but through the windows the sunlight illuminated my parents' bedroom. Sandy and I came in to talk to him, both of us shy and grateful and, of course, stunned by how helpless he appeared seated weakly in a lone chair in the corner of the room. Seeing his sons together like that, my father could no longer control himself and began to sob. He was alive, the sun was shining, his wife was not widowed nor his boys fatherless—family life would now resume. It was not so complicated that an eleven-year-old couldn't understand his father's tears. I just didn't see, as he so clearly could, why or how it should have turned out differently.

I knew only two boys in our neighborhood whose families were fatherless, and thought of them as no less blighted than the blind girl who attended our school for a while and had to be read to and shepherded everywhere. The fatherless boys seemed almost equally marked and set apart; in the aftermath of their fathers' deaths, they too struck me as scary and a little taboo. Though one was a model of obedience and the other a troublemaker, everything either of them did or said seemed determined by his being a boy with a dead father and, however innocently I arrived at this notion, I was probably right.

I knew no child whose family was divided by divorce. Outside of the movie magazines and the tabloid headlines, it didn't exist, certainly not among Jews like us. Jews didn't get divorced—not because divorce was forbidden by Jewish law but because that was the way they were. If Jewish fathers didn't come home drunk and beat their wives—and in our neighborhood, which was Jewry to me, I'd never heard of any who did—that too was because of the way they were. In our lore, the Jewish family was an inviolate haven against every form of menace, from personal isolation to gentile hostility. Regardless of internal friction and strife, it was assumed to be an indissoluble consolidation. *Hear, O Israel, the family is God, the family is One.*

Family indivisibility, the first commandment.

In the late 1940s, when my father's younger brother, Bernie, proclaimed his intention of divorcing the wife of nearly twenty years who was the mother of his two daughters, my mother and father were as stunned as if they'd heard that he'd killed somebody. Had Bernie committed murder and gone to jail for life, they would probably have rallied behind him despite the abominable, inexplicable deed. But when he made up his mind not merely to divorce but to do so to marry a younger woman, their support went instantly to the "victims," the sister-in-law and the nieces. For his transgression, a breach of faith with his wife, his children, his entire clan—a dereliction of his duty as a Jew *and* as a Roth—Bernie encountered virtually universal condemnation.

That family rupture only began to mend when time revealed that no one had been destroyed by the divorce; in fact, anguished as they were by the breakup of their household, Bernie's ex-wife and his two girls were never remotely as indignant as the rest of the relatives. The healing owed a lot to Bernie himself, a more diplomatic man than most of his judges, but also to the fact that for my father the demands of family solidarity and the bond of family history exceeded even *his* admonishing instincts. It was to be another forty-odd years, however, before the two brothers threw their arms around each other and hungrily embraced in an unmistakable act of unqualified reconciliation. This occurred a few weeks before Bernie's death, in his late seventies, when his heart was failing rapidly and nobody, beginning with himself, expected him to last much longer.

I had driven my father over to see Bernie and his wife, Ruth, in their condominium in a retirement village in northwestern Connecticut, twenty miles from my own home. It was Bernie's turn now to wear the little face of his unillusioned, stoical old mother; when he came to the door to let us in, there in his features was that stark resemblance that seemed to emerge in all the Roth brothers when they were up against it.

Ordinarily the two men would have met with a handshake, but when my father stepped into the hallway, so much was clear both about the time that was left to Bernie and about all those decades, seemingly stretching back to the beginning of time, during which they had been alive as their parents' offspring, that the handshake was swallowed up in a forceful hug that lasted minutes and left them in tears. They seemed to be saying goodbye to everyone already gone as well as to each other, the last two surviving children of the dour hat-blocker Sender and the imperturbable *balabusta* Bertha. Safely in his brother's arms, Bernie seemed also to be saying goodbye to himself. There was nothing to guard against or defend against or resent anymore, nothing even to remember. In these brothers, men so deeply swayed, despite their dissimilarity, by identical strains of family emotion, everything remembered had been distilled into pure, barely bearable feeling.

In the car afterward my father said, "We haven't held each other like that since we were small boys. My brother's dying, Philip. I used to push him around in his carriage. There were nine of us, with my mother and father. I'll be the last one left."

While we drove back to my house (where he was staying in the upstairs back bedroom, a room in which he says he never fails to sleep like a baby) he recounted the struggles of each of his five brothers—with bankruptcies, illnesses, and in-laws, with marital dissension and bad loans, and with children, with their Gonerils, their Regans, and their Cordelias. He recalled for me the martyrdom of his only sister, what she and all the family had gone through when her husband the bookkeeper who liked the horses had served a little time for embezzlement.

It wasn't exactly the first time I was hearing these stories. Narrative is the form that his knowledge takes, and his repertoire has never been large: family, family, family, Newark, Newark, Newark, Jew, Jew, Jew. Somewhat like mine.

I naïvely believed as a child that I would always have a father present, and the truth seems to be that I always will. However awkward the union may sometimes have been, vulnerable to differences of opinion, to false expectations, to radically divergent experiences of America, strained by the colliding of two impatient, equally willful temperaments and marred by masculine clumsiness, the link to him has been omnipresent. What's more, now, when he no longer com-

mands my attention by his bulging biceps and his moral strictures, now, when he is no longer the biggest man I have to
contend with—and when I am not all that far from being an
old man myself—I am able to laugh at his jokes and hold his
hand and concern myself with his well-being, I'm able to love
him the way I wanted to when I was sixteen, seventeen, and
eighteen but when, what with dealing with him and feeling
at odds with him, it was simply an impossibility. *The* impossibility, for all that I always respected him for his particular
burden and his struggle within a system that he didn't choose.
The mythological role of a Jewish boy growing up in a family
like mine—to become the hero one's father failed to be—I
may even have achieved by now, but not at all in the way
that was preordained. After nearly forty years of living far
from home, I'm equipped at last to be the most loving of
sons—just, however, when he has another agenda. He is
trying to die. He doesn't say that, nor, probably, does he
think of it in those words, but that's his job now and, fight as
he will to survive, he understands, as he always has, what the
real work is.

Trying to die isn't like trying to commit suicide—it may
actually be harder, because what you are trying to do is what
you least want to have happen; you dread it but there it is
and it must be done, and by no one but you. Twice in the
last few years he has taken a shot at it, on two different
occasions suddenly became so ill that I, who was then living
abroad half the year, flew back to America to find him with
barely enough strength to walk from the sofa to the TV set
without clutching at every chair in between. And though each
time the doctor, after a painstaking examination, was unable
to find anything wrong with him, he nonetheless went to bed
every night expecting not to awaken in the morning and, when
he did awaken in the morning, he was fifteen minutes just

getting himself into a sitting position on the edge of the bed and another hour shaving and dressing. Then, for God knows how long, he slouched unmoving over a bowl of cereal for which he had absolutely no appetite.

I was as certain as he was that this was it, yet neither time could he pull it off and, over a period of weeks, he recovered his strength and became himself again, loathing Reagan, defending Israel, phoning relatives, attending funerals, writing to newspapers, castigating William Buckley, watching MacNeil–Lehrer, exhorting his grown grandchildren, remembering in detail our own dead, and relentlessly, exactingly— and without having been asked—monitoring the caloric intake of the nice woman he lives with. It would seem that to prevail here, to try dying and to *do* it, he will have to work even harder than he did in the insurance business, where he achieved a remarkable success for a man with his social and educational handicaps. Of course, here too he'll eventually succeed—though clearly, despite his record of assiduous application to every job he has ever been assigned, things won't be easy. But then they never have been.

Needless to say, the link to my father was never so voluptuously tangible as the colossal bond to my mother's flesh, whose metamorphosed incarnation was a sleek black sealskin coat into which I, the younger, the privileged, the pampered papoose, blissfully wormed myself whenever my father chauffeured us home to New Jersey on a winter Sunday from our semiannual excursion to Radio City Music Hall and Manhattan's Chinatown: the unnameable animal-me bearing her dead father's name, the protoplasm-me, boy-baby, and body-burrower-in-training, joined by every nerve ending to her smile and her sealskin coat, while his resolute dutifulness, his relentless industriousness, his unreasoning obstinacy and harsh resentments, his illusions, his innocence, his allegiances, his fears were to constitute the original mold for the American, Jew, citizen, man, even for the writer, I would become. To be at all is to be her Philip, but in the embroilment with the buffeting world, my history still takes its spin from beginning as his Roth.

Safe at Home

The greatest menace while I was growing up came from abroad, from the Germans and the Japanese, our enemies because we were American. I still remember my terror as a nine-year-old when, running in from playing on the street after school, I saw the banner headline CORREGIDOR FALLS on the evening paper in our doorway and understood that the United States actually could lose the war it had entered only months before. At home the biggest threat came from the Americans who opposed or resisted us—or condescended to us or rigorously excluded us—because we were Jews. Though I knew that we were tolerated and accepted as well—in publicized individual cases, even specially esteemed—and though I never doubted that this country was mine (and New Jersey and Newark as well), I was not unaware of the power to intimidate that emanated from the highest and lowest reaches of gentile America.

At the top were the gentile executives who ran my father's company, the Metropolitan Life, from the home office at Number One Madison Avenue (the first Manhattan street address I ever knew). When I was a small boy, my father, then in his early thirties, was still a new Metropolitan agent, working a six-day week, including most evenings, and grateful for the steady, if modest, living this job provided, even during the Depression; a family shoe store he'd opened after marrying my mother had gone bankrupt some years before, and in between he'd had to take a variety of low-paying, unpromising jobs. He proudly explained to his sons that the Metropolitan was "the largest financial institution in the world" and that as an agent he provided Metropolitan Life policyholders with "an umbrella for a rainy day." The company put out dozens of pamphlets to educate its policyholders about health and disease; I collected a new batch off the racks in the waiting room on Saturday mornings when he took me along with him to the narrow downtown street where the Essex district office of Newark occupied nearly a whole floor of a commercial office building. I read up on "Tuberculosis," "Pregnancy," and "Diabetes," while he labored over his ledger entries and his paperwork. Sometimes at his desk, impressing myself by sitting in his swivel chair, I practiced my penmanship on Metropolitan stationery; in one corner of the paper was my father's name and in the other a picture of the home-office tower, topped with the beacon that he described to me, in the Metropolitan's own phrase, as the light that never failed.

In our apartment a framed replica of the Declaration of Independence hung above the telephone table on the hallway wall—it had been awarded by the Metropolitan to the men of my father's district for a successful year in the field, and seeing it there daily during my first school years forged an association between the venerated champions of equality who signed that cherished document and our benefactors, the corporate fathers at Number One Madison Avenue, where the reigning president was, fortuitously, a Mr. Lincoln. If that wasn't enough, the home-office executive whom my father would trek from New Jersey to see when his star began to rise slightly in the company was the superintendent of agencies, a Mr. Wright, whose good opinion my father valued inordinately all his life and whose height and imposing good looks he admired nearly as much as he did the man's easygoing diplomacy. As my father's son I felt no less respectful toward these awesomely named gentiles than he did, but I, like him, knew that they had to be the very officials who openly and guiltlessly conspired to prevent more than a few token Jews from assuming positions of anything approaching importance within the largest financial institution in the world.

One reason my father so admired the Jewish manager of his own district, Sam Peterfreund—aside, of course, from the devotion that Peterfreund inspired by recognizing my father's drive early on and making him an assistant manager—was that Peterfreund had climbed to the leadership of such a large, productive office despite the company's deep-rooted reluctance to allow a Jew to rise too high. When Mr. Peterfreund was to make one of his rare visits for dinner, the green felt protective pads came out of the hall closet and were laid by my brother and me on the dining room table, it was spread with a fresh linen cloth and linen napkins, water goblets appeared, and we ate off "the good dishes" in the dining room, where there hung a large oil painting of a floral arrangement, copied skillfully from the Louvre by my mother's brother, Mickey; on the sideboard were framed photographic portraits of the two dead men for whom I'd been named, my mother's father, Philip, and my father's younger brother, Milton. We ate in the dining room only on religious holidays, on special family occasions, and when Mr. Peterfreund came—and we all called him Mr. Peterfreund, even when he wasn't there; my father also addressed him directly as "Boss." "Want a drink, Boss?" Before dinner we sat unnaturally, like guests in our own living room, while Mr. Peterfreund sipped his schnapps and I was encouraged to listen to his wisdom. The esteem he inspired was a tribute to a gentile-sanctioned Jew managing a big Metropolitan office as much as to an immediate supervisor whose goodwill determined my father's occupational well-being and our family fate. A large, bald-headed man with a gold chain across his vest and a slightly mysterious German accent, whose family lived (in high style, I imagined) in New York (*and* on Long Island) while (no less glamorously to me) he slept during the week in a Newark hotel, the Boss was our family's Bernard Baruch.

Opposition more frightening than corporate discrimination came from the lowest reaches of the gentile world, from the gangs of *lumpen* kids who, one summer, swarmed out of Neptune, a ramshackle little town on the Jersey shore, and stampeded along the boardwalk into Bradley Beach, hollering "Kikes! Dirty Jews!" and beating up whoever hadn't run for cover. Bradley Beach, a couple of miles south of Asbury Park on the mid-Jersey coast, was the very modest little vacation resort where we and hundreds of other lower-middle-class Jews from humid, mosquito-ridden north Jersey cities rented rooms or shared small bungalows for several weeks during the summer. It was paradise for me, even though we lived three in a room, and four when my father drove down the old Cheesequake highway to see us on weekends or to stay for his two-week vacation. In all of my intensely secure and protected childhood, I don't believe I ever felt more exuberantly snug than I did in those mildly anarchic rooming houses, where—inevitably with more strain than valor—some ten or twelve women tried to share the shelves of a single large icebox, and to cook side by side, in a crowded communal kitchen, for children, visiting husbands, and elderly parents. Meals were eaten in the unruly, kibbutzlike atmosphere—so unlike the ambiance in my own orderly home—of the underventilated dining room.

The hot, unhomelike, homey hubbub of the Bradley Beach rooming house was somberly contrasted, in the early forties, by reminders all along the shore that the country was fighting in an enormous war: bleak, barbwired Coast Guard bunkers dotted the beaches, and scores of lonely, very young sailors played the amusement machines in the arcades at Asbury Park; the lights were blacked out along the boardwalk at night and the blackout shades on the rooming-house windows made it stifling indoors after dinner; there was even tarry refuse, alleged to be from torpedoed ships, that washed up and littered the beach—I sometimes had fears of wading gleefully with my friends into the surf and bumping against the body of someone killed at sea. Also—and most peculiarly, since we were all supposed to be pulling together to beat the Axis Powers—there were these "race riots," as we children called the hostile nighttime invasions by the boys from Neptune: violence directed against the Jews by youngsters who, as everyone said, could only have learned their hatred from what they heard at home.

Though the riots occurred just twice, for much of one July and August it was deemed unwise for a Jewish child to venture out after supper alone, or even with friends, though nighttime freedom in shorts and sandals was one of Bradley's greatest pleasures for a ten-year-old on vacation from homework and the school year's bedtime hours. The morning after the first riot, a story spread among the kids collecting Popsicle sticks and playing ring-a-lievo on the Lorraine Avenue beach; it was about somebody (whom nobody seemed to know personally) who had been caught before he could get away: the anti-Semites had held him down and pulled his face back and forth across the splintery surface of the boardwalk's weathered planks. This particular horrific detail, whether apocryphal or not—and it needn't necessarily have been—impressed upon me how barbaric was this irrational hatred of families who, as anyone could see, were simply finding in Bradley Beach a little inexpensive relief from the city heat, people just trying to have a quiet good time, bothering no one, except occasionally each other, as when one of the women purportedly expropriated from the icebox, for her family's corn on the cob, somebody else's quarter of a pound of salt butter. If that was as much harm as any of us could do, why make a bloody pulp of a Jewish child's face?

The home-office gentiles in executive positions at Number One Madison Avenue were hardly comparable to the kids swarming into Bradley screaming "Kike!"; and yet when I thought about it, I saw that they were no more reasonable or fair: they too were against Jews for no good reason. Small wonder that at twelve, when I was advised to begin to think seriously about what I would do when I grew up, I decided to oppose the injustices wreaked by the violent and the privileged by becoming a lawyer for the underdog.

When I entered high school, the menace shifted to School Stadium, then the only large football grounds in Newark, situated on alien Bloomfield Avenue, a forty-minute bus ride from Weequahic High. On Saturdays in the fall, four of the city's seven high schools would meet in a doubleheader, as many as two thousand kids pouring in for the first game, which began around noon, and then emptying en masse into the surrounding streets when the second game had ended in the falling shadows. It was inevitable after a hard-fought game

that intense school rivalries would culminate in a brawl some-
where in the stands and that, in an industrial city of strongly
divergent ethnic backgrounds and subtle, though pronounced, class gradations, fights would break out among vol-
atile teenagers from four very different neighborhoods. Yet
the violence provoked by the presence of a Weequahic
crowd—particularly after a rare Weequahic victory—was unlike any other.

I remember being in the stands with my friends in my
sophomore year, rooting uninhibitedly for the "Indians," as
our Weequahic teams were known in the Newark sports pages;
after never having beaten Barringer High in the fourteen years
of Weequahic's existence, our team was leading them 6–0 in
the waning minutes of the Columbus Day game. The Barringer backfield was Berry, Peloso, Short, and Thompson; in the
Weequahic backfield were Weissman, Weiss, Gold, and full-
back Fred Rosenberg, who'd led a sustained march down the
field at the end of the first half and then, on a two-yard plunge,
had scored what Fred, now a PR consultant in New Jersey,
recently wrote to tell me was "one of the only touchdowns
notched by the Indians that entire season, on a run that probably was one of the longer runs from scrimmage in 1947."

As the miraculous game was nearing its end—as Barringer,
tied with Central for first place in the City League, was about
to be upset by the weakest high school team in Newark—I
suddenly noticed that the rival fans on the other side of the
stadium bowl had begun to stream down the aisles, making
their way around the far ends of the stadium toward us. Instead of waiting for the referee's final whistle, I bolted for an
exit and, along with nearly everyone else who understood
what was happening, ran down the stadium ramp in the direction of the buses waiting to take us back to our neighborhood. Though there were a number of policemen around, it

was easy to see that once the rampage was under way, unless you were clinging to a cop with both arms and both legs, his protection wouldn't be much help; should you be caught on your own by a gang from one of the other three schools waiting to get their hands on a Weequahic Jew—our school was almost entirely Jewish—it was unlikely that you'd emerge from the stadium without serious injury.

The nearest bus was already almost full when I made it on board; as soon as the last few kids shoved their way in, the uniformed Public Service driver, fearful for his own safety as a transporter of Weequahic kids, drew the front door shut. By then there were easily ten or fifteen of the enemy, aged twelve to twenty, surrounding the bus and hammering their fists against its sides. Fred Rosenberg contends that "every able-bodied man from north Newark, his brother, and their offspring got into the act." When one of them, having worked his hands through a crevice under the window beside my seat, started forcing the window up with his fingers, I grabbed it from the top and brought it down as hard as I could. He howled and somebody took a swing at the window with a baseball bat, breaking the frame but miraculously not the glass. Before the others could join together to tear back the door, board the bus, and go straight for me—who would have been hard put to explain that the reprisal had been uncharacteristic and intended only in self-defense—the driver had pulled out from the curb and we were safely away from the postgame pogrom, which, for our adversaries, constituted perhaps the most enjoyable part of the day's entertainment.

That evening I fled again, not only because I was a fourteen-year-old weighing only a little over a hundred pounds but because I was never to be one of the few who stayed behind for a fight but always among the many whose impulse is to run to avoid it. A boy in our neighborhood might be expected to protect himself in a schoolyard confrontation with another boy his age and size, but no stigma attached to taking flight from a violent melee—by and large it was considered both shameful and stupid for a bright Jewish child to get caught up in something so dangerous to his physical safety, and so repugnant to Jewish instincts. The collective memory of Polish and Russian pogroms had fostered in most of our families the idea that our worth as human beings, even perhaps our distinction as a people, was embodied in the *incapacity* to perpetrate the sort of bloodletting visited upon our ancestors.

For a while during my adolescence I studiously followed prizefighting, could recite the names and weights of all the champions and contenders, and even subscribed briefly to *Ring*, Nat Fleischer's colorful boxing magazine. As kids my brother and I had been taken by our father to the local boxing arena, where invariably we all had a good time. From my father and his friends I heard about the prowess of Benny Leonard, Barney Ross, Max Baer, and the clownishly nicknamed Slapsie Maxie Rosenbloom. And yet Jewish boxers and boxing aficionados remained, like boxing itself, "sport" in the bizarre sense, a strange deviation from the norm and interesting largely for that reason: in the world whose values first formed me, unrestrained physical aggression was considered contemptible everywhere else. I could no more smash a nose with a fist than fire a pistol into someone's heart. And what imposed this restraint, if not on Slapsie Maxie Rosenbloom, then on me, was my being Jewish. In my scheme of things, Slapsie Maxie was a more miraculous Jewish phenomenon by far than Dr. Albert Einstein.

The evening following our escape from School Stadium the ritual victory bonfire was held on the dirt playing field on Chancellor Avenue, across from Syd's, a popular Weequahic hangout where my brother and I each did part-time stints selling hot dogs and french fries. I'd virtually evolved as a boy on that playing field; it was two blocks from my house and bordered on the grade school—"Chancellor Avenue"—that I'd attended for eight years, which itself stood next to Weequahic High. It was the field where I'd played pickup football and baseball, where my brother had competed in school track meets, where I'd shagged flies for hours with anybody who would fungo the ball out to me, where my friends and I hung around on Sunday mornings, watching with amusement as the local fathers—the plumbers, the electricians, the produce merchants—kibitzed their way through their weekly softball game. If ever I had been called on to express my love for my neighborhood in a single reverential act, I couldn't have done better than to get down on my hands and knees and kiss the ground behind home plate.

Yet upon this, the sacred heart of my inviolate homeland, our stadium attackers launched a nighttime raid, the conclusion to the violence begun that afternoon, their mopping-up exercise. A few hours after the big fire had been lit, as we happily sauntered around the dark field, joking among ourselves and looking for girls to impress, while in the distance the cartwheeling cheerleaders led the chant of the crowd encircling the fire—"And when you're up against Weequahic/ you're upside down!"—the cars pulled up swiftly on Chancellor Avenue, and the same guys who'd been pounding on the sides of my bus (or so I quickly assumed) were racing onto the field, some of them waving baseball bats. The field was set into the slope of the Chancellor Avenue hill; I ran through the dark to the nearest wall, jumped some six feet down into Hobson Street, and then just kept going, through alleyways, between garages, and over backyard fences, until I'd made it safely home in less than five minutes. One of my Leslie Street friends, the football team water boy, who'd been standing in the full glare of the fire wearing his Weequahic varsity jacket, was not so quick or lucky; his assailants—identified in the neighborhood the next day as "Italians"—picked him up and threw him bodily toward the flames. He landed just at the fire's edge and, though he wasn't burned, spent days in the hospital recovering from internal injuries.

But this was a unique calamity. Our lower-middle-class neighborhood of houses and shops—a few square miles of tree-lined streets at the corner of the city bordering on residential Hillside and semi-industrial Irvington—was as safe and peaceful a haven for me as his rural community would have been for an Indiana farm boy. Ordinarily nobody more disquieting ever appeared there than the bearded old Jew who sometimes tapped on our door around dinnertime; to me an unnerving specter from the harsh and distant European past, he stood silently in the dim hallway while I went to get a quarter to drop into his collection can for the Jewish National Fund (a name that never sank all the way in: the only nation for Jews, as I saw it, was the democracy to which I was so loyally—and lyrically—bound, regardless of the unjust bias of the so-called best and the violent hatred of some of the worst). Shapiro, the immigrant tailor who also did dry cleaning, had two thumbs on one hand, and that made bringing our clothes to him a little eerie for me when I was still small. And there was LeRoy "the moron," a somewhat gruesome but innocuous neighborhood dimwit who gave me the creeps when he sat down on the front stoop to listen to a bunch of us talking after school. On our street he was rarely teased but just sat looking at us stupidly with his hollow eyes and rhythmically tapping one foot—and that was about as frightening as things ever got.

A typical memory is of five or six of us energetically traversing the whole length of the neighborhood Friday nights on our way back from a double feature at the Roosevelt Theater. We would stop off at the Watson Bagel Company on Clinton Place to buy, for a few pennies each, a load of the first warm bagels out of the oven—and this was four decades before the bagel became a breakfast staple at Burger King. Devouring three and four apiece, we'd circuitously walk one another home, howling with laughter at our jokes and imitating our favorite baritones. When the weather was good we'd sometimes wind up back of Chancellor Avenue School, on the wooden bleachers along the sidelines of the asphalt playground adjacent to the big dirt playing field. Stretched on our backs in the open night air, we were as carefree as any kids anywhere in postwar America, and certainly we felt ourselves no less American. Discussions about Jewishness and being Jewish, which I was to hear so often among intellectual Jews once I was an adult in Chicago and New York, were altogether unknown; we talked about being misunderstood by our families, about movies and radio programs and sex and sports, we even argued about politics, though this was rare since our fathers were all ardent New Dealers and there was no disagreement among us about the sanctity of F.D.R. and the Democratic Party. About being Jewish there was nothing more to say than there was about having two arms and two legs. It would have seemed to us strange *not* to be Jewish—stranger still, to hear someone announce that he wished he weren't a Jew or that he intended not to be in the future.

Yet, simultaneously, this intense adolescent camaraderie was the primary means by which we were deepening our *Americanness*. Our parents were, with few exceptions, the first-generation offspring of poor turn-of-the-century immigrants from Galicia and Polish Russia, raised in predominantly Yiddish-speaking Newark households where religious Orthodoxy was only just beginning to be seriously eroded by American life. However unaccented and American-sounding their speech, however secularized their own beliefs, and adept and convincing their American style of lower-middle-class existence, they were influenced still by their childhood training and by strong parental ties to what often seemed to us antiquated, socially useless old-country mores and perceptions.

My larger boyhood society cohered around the most inherently American phenomenon at hand—the game of baseball, whose mystique was encapsulated in three relatively inexpensive fetishes that you could have always at your side in your room, not only while you did your homework but in bed with you while you slept if you were a worshiper as primitive as I was at ten and eleven: they were a ball, a bat, and a glove. The solace that my Orthodox grandfather doubtless took in the familiar leathery odor of the flesh-worn straps of the old phylacteries in which he wrapped himself each morning, I derived from the smell of my mitt, which I ritualistically donned every day to work a little on my pocket. I was an average playground player, and the mitt's enchantment had to do less with foolish dreams of becoming a major leaguer, or even a high school star, than with the bestowal of membership in a great secular nationalistic church from which nobody had ever seemed to suggest that Jews should be excluded. (The blacks were another story, until 1947.) The softball and hardball teams we organized and reorganized obsessively throughout our grade-school years—teams we called by unarguably native names like the Seabees and the Mohawks and described as "social and athletic clubs"—aside from the opportunity they afforded to compete against one another in a game we loved, also operated as secret societies that separated us from the faint, residual foreignness still clinging to some of our parents' attitudes and that validated our own spotless credentials as American kids. Paradoxically, our remotely recent old-country Jewish origins may well have been a source of our especially intense devotion to a sport that, unlike boxing or even football, had nothing to do with the menace of brute force unleashed against flesh and bones.

The Weequahic neighborhood for over two decades now has been part of the vast black Newark slum. Visiting my father in Elizabeth, I'll occasionally take a roundabout route off the parkway into my old Newark and, to give myself an emotional workout, drive through the streets still entirely familiar to me despite the boarded-up shops and badly decaying houses, and the knowledge that my white face is not at all welcome. Recently, snaking back and forth in my car along the one-way streets of the Weequahic section, I began to imagine house plaques commemorating the achievements of the boys who'd once lived there, markers of the kind you see in London and Paris on the residences of the historically renowned. What I inscribed on those plaques, along with my friends' names and their years of birth and of local residence, wasn't the professional status they had attained in later life but the position each had played on those neighborhood teams of ours in the 1940s. I thought that if you knew that in this four-family Hobson Street house there once lived the third baseman Seymour Feldman and that down a few doors had lived Ronnie Rubin, who in his boyhood had been our catcher, you'd understand how and where the Feldman and the Rubin families had been naturalized irrevocably by their young sons.

In 1982, while I was visiting my widowered father in Miami Beach during his first season there on his own, I got him one night to walk over with me to Meyer Lansky's old base of operations, the Hotel Singapore on Collins Avenue; earlier in the day he'd told me that wintering at the Singapore were some of the last of his generation from our neighborhood— the ones, he mordantly added, "still aboveground." Among the faces I recognized in the lobby, where the elderly residents met to socialize each evening after dinner, was the mother of one of the boys who also used to play ball incessantly "up the field" and who hung around on the playground bleachers after dark back when we were Seabees together. As we sat talking at the edge of a gin-rummy game, she suddenly took hold of my hand and, smiling at me with deeply emotional eyes—with that special heart-filled look that *all* our mothers had—she said, "Phil, the feeling there was among you boys— I've never seen anything like it again." I told her, altogether truthfully, that I haven't either.

Joe College

Working as an assistant manager in the Essex district office of Metropolitan Life, my father earned, during his best years, about $125 a week in salary and commissions. In the middle 1940s, as I made the transition from grade school to high school, a business risk he took wiped out the family savings. After long consultations with my mother, he had invested with some friends in a frozen-food distribution company, and for several years he continued by day as a Metropolitan insurance man while at night and on weekends, without drawing a salary, he went out on the refrigerated truck, trying to hustle frozen-food business in Jersey and eastern Pennsylvania. In addition to using up the family savings he'd had to borrow some $8,000 from relatives in order to pay for his share in the partnership. He was forty-five, and took the risk because it seemed unlikely that, being Jewish, he could get any further with the Met-

ropolitan. His education, through eighth grade, also seemed
to him an impediment to promotion.

He had hoped that by the time his two sons graduated from
high school, the new enterprise would have taken off and he'd
be able to afford to send us both to college. But the business
went bust quickly, and when I was ready for college, he was
still saddled with paying off his debt. Fortunately, in 1949 he
was unexpectedly promoted by the Metropolitan to manage
an office just outside Newark, in Union City. The district was
doing virtually no business when he came in but offered a
real financial opportunity if he could somehow inspire the
hapless agency with his know-how and energy. As it happened, he was spared the expense of my brother's college
education by the GI Bill. In 1946, with the war draft still on,
Sandy had gone into the Navy, and when he came out, in
1948, he was able to attend art school in Brooklyn without
help from the family. I graduated from high school in January
of 1950 and worked as a stock clerk in a Newark department
store until I enrolled, in September, as a prelaw student, at
Newark Colleges of Rutgers, the unprestigious little downtown branch of the state university. I had wanted desperately
to go away to college, if only to the Rutgers main campus,
down in New Brunswick, but though I had graduated at sixteen well up in my class, I'd been unable to win a Rutgers
scholarship. I wound up as a freshman in Newark, still living
at home.

My dream of *away* remained fervent, however satisfied I
actually found myself at Newark Rutgers, which was situated
a little beyond the city's commercial district at the "historic"
end of the downtown streets, about a twenty-minute bus ride
from my corner. It felt invigoratingly grown-up to be downtown not as a kid going to the movies with his friends or a
boy out to Sunday dinner with his family or a lowly stock clerk

mindlessly pushing a rack around S. Klein's, but as the owner of spanking-new textbooks, with a businesslike briefcase (for his lunch) and a pipe in his pocket that he was learning to smoke. It appealed to my liberal democratic spirit to be taking college courses in a building that had once been a brewery and to be seated there alongside Italian and Irish kids from city high schools that had been foreign, unknowable, even unnervingly hostile to me when I was attending a neighborhood school whose student body was more than ninety percent Jewish. I considered it a kind of triumphant liberation to have been drawn into the city's rivalrous ethnic society, especially as our liberal-arts studies were working—in my idealistic vision—to elevate us above serious social differences, to free from cultural narrowness and intellectual impoverishment the offspring of Weequahic's Jewish businessmen as well as working-class boys from the Ironbound district. Casually making friends over paper-bag lunches with gentile classmates who had graduated from Barringer and South Side and Central and West Side—boys who previously had been nothing more to me than tough and generally superior adversaries in intercity sporting events—made me feel expansively "American." I hadn't any doubts that we Jews were already American or that the Weequahic section was anything other than a quintessentially American urban neighborhood, but as a child of the war and of the brotherhood mythology embodied in songs like Frank Sinatra's "The House I Live In" and Tony Martin's "Tenement Symphony," I was exhilarated to feel in contact with the country's much-proclaimed, self-defining heterogeneity.

At the same time, I knew that if I remained in our five-room flat on Leslie Street, living and studying in the bedroom that I had shared since earliest childhood with my brother, there would be increasing friction between my father and me, simply because I could no longer truthfully account to him, or to my mother, either—though she would never dare ask—for my weekend whereabouts or my Saturday-night hours. I was quite tame, a good, responsible boy with good, responsible friends; I couldn't have been more dutiful and well mannered, and lacked anything resembling unconstrainable impulses; but I was also strong-minded and independent, and if my father were to challenge the ordering of my private life, now that I was a college student, I would feel suffocated by his strictures. I had also outgrown the family dinner table and was as impatient as any rapidly maturing adolescent with my parents' conversation, but the main reason that I wanted to get away from home for my sophomore year was to protect a hardworking, self-sacrificing father and a devoted but determined son from a battle that they were equally ill equipped to fight.

My mother was really no problem. As soon as my brother and I started giving genuine signs of burgeoning independence, she had relaxed the exacting, sometimes overly fastidious strictures that had governed our early upbringing and began to be mildly intimidated by our airs of maturity; in a way she fell in love with us all over again, like a shy schoolgirl this time, hoping for a date. It was a rather prototypic kind of movement, I think, for the mother to go from nurturing her sons to being a little afraid of them and for the sons to move out of their mother's province at thirteen or fourteen. Sandy—born when she was twenty-three, a pretty, very innocent young woman in a penniless marriage whose own girlhood had been rigorously overseen by a stern, tyrannical father—seems as a child to have felt more constrained by her vigilant mothering than I ever did, though he, no less than I, found more than a little sustenance in the inexhaustible maternal feeling that visibly instigated and tenderized that conscientiousness. Still and all, he may well have endured a more inflexible regimen, more assiduously imposed, than what befell me, coming five years later, after she'd had the education of raising him and when my father's weekly Metropolitan paycheck had begun to mitigate their financial anxieties. To me, at eight, nine, and ten, home had seemed just perfect, but that was no longer so at sixteen and I wanted to get away.

I didn't care where "away" was—one college would do as well as another. All I needed were professors and courses and a library. I'd study hard, get a "good education," and go on to become the idealistic lawyer I'd imagined becoming since I was twelve. Since none of my immediate relatives had ever graduated from a liberal-arts college, there was no one to point me in the direction of his alma mater. And because of the war and the postwar draft, the generation of college-educated younger men whose example I might have followed had disappeared from the neighborhood entirely; when they showed up again, they were veterans on the GI Bill who seemed vastly older and unapproachable. Our only real tutors were the ex-GIs—the rumba dancers and service-station attendants, the make-out artists, soda jerks, and short-order cooks—who had little to do but hang around and play pickup basketball with us. Under the bleachers of the playground they taught us how to shoot craps and to play five-card stud with change stolen from our mothers' purses and our fathers' trouser pockets; but as for college guidance, I knew I had better look elsewhere.

My brother had been a Saturday student at the Art Students League in New York during his high school days and, after his discharge from the Navy, spent three years at Pratt Institute. While I was finishing high school, he would come home from Pratt on weekends to set up his easel in the dining room and, over a thick layer of old newspapers, lay out his paints and his drawing materials on the dining-room table; sometimes he would leave behind copies of paperback books he'd been reading on the subway and the train home. That's how, at fifteen and sixteen, I came to read *Winesburg, Ohio* and *A Portrait of the Artist* and *Only the Dead Know Brooklyn*. He drew from nude models, he had his own apartment, as a sailor he'd sat in bars where there were whores, and now he did quick, expressive pen-and-ink sketches of Bowery bums. But great as my admiration was for these achievements, Sandy's mode wasn't one I could simply emulate: his studies were preparing him for a career as an artist, while my talent, as described in the family, was "the gift of the gab."

In grade school I'd been taken once by my Uncle Ed, a cardboard-carton dealer, to see a football game at Princeton. I had not forgotten the campus—either the green quadrangles or the evocative word—yet it would never have occurred to me to apply there. I knew from my uncle that despite the presence of Einstein, to whose house we'd made a pilgrimage, Princeton didn't "take Jews." (That's why we'd rooted so hard for Rutgers.) As for Harvard and Yale, not only did they seem, like Princeton, to be bastions of the gentile upper crust, socially too exclusive and unsympathetic, but their admissions officers were revealed by the Anti-Defamation League of B'nai B'rith to employ "Jewish quotas," a practice that disgusted a patriotic young American (let alone a member of an ineluctably Jewish family) like me. A champion of the Four Freedoms, a foe of the DAR, a supporter of Henry Wallace. I detested the idea of privilege that these famously elitist colleges, with their discriminatory policies, seemed to symbolize. Though I don't think I could have expressed this then in so many words, I certainly didn't want to recapitulate, at Harvard or Yale, my father's struggle at the Metropolitan to succeed with an institution holding a long-standing belief in Protestant Anglo-

Saxon superiority. What's more, if I couldn't win a scholarship to Rutgers, how could I expect assistance from the Ivy League?

There were other colleges, anyway, hundreds of them: Wake Forest, Bowling Green, Clemson, Allegheny, Baylor, Vanderbilt, Bowdoin, Colby, Tulane—I knew their names, if nothing more (not even precisely where all of them were), from listening to Stan Lomax and Bill Stern announce the football scores on the radio Saturday nights throughout the fall. I read the names of these places on the sports pages of the *Newark Evening News* and the *Newark Sunday Call* and saw them on the football-pool cards that you could buy at the candy store on our corner for as little as a quarter. The football pool was illegal—run, my father told me, by Longy Zwillman and the Newark mob—but I began to buy the cards when I was about eleven and, with a couple of other neighborhood kids, started selling them on the school playground for the candy-store owner when I was thirteen, establishing my sole affiliation ever with organized crime. Through the pool I probably became familiar with far more institutions of higher learning than was the college adviser at the high school, who had suggested to me, when I admitted I might actually like to become a journalist rather than a lawyer, that I should apply to the University of Missouri. When I told my parents her advice, my mother looked flabbergasted. "Missouri," my mother repeated tragically. "They have a great journalism school," I told her. "You're not going to Missouri," my father informed me. "It's too far and we can't afford it."

It was during Christmas vacation from Newark Rutgers that I got to talking to my Leslie Street neighbor Marty Castlebaum, with whom I'd had a genial, if not particularly intimate, friendship ever since grade school. Marty, who is now a physician in New Jersey, was something of a loner—a skinny,

very tall boy, seemingly not so obsessed with sex or so romantically adventurous as my best friends. He was a good,
quiet student with an enthusiasm for baseball, very much the
product of a respectable, secularized Jewish family. The Cas-
tlebaums' outward configuration—and household orderli-
ness—resembled my own family's: a highly competent and
well-mannered mother, a hardworking, forthright father (a
lawyer, however, and so a big vocational notch up from mine),
and an older brother whom Marty strikingly resembled.
Though there was something cheery in his temperate character I'd always liked, I found him more housebound than
the boys to whom I was closest. If I remember correctly,
Marty practiced the piano with real devotion, which in my
mind may have separated him a little too much from those of
us who counterbalanced good grades and courteous conduct
with shooting craps on the sly and (against the unlikely possibility of being called upon to produce one) storing sealed
Trojans in our wallets. His family lived even closer to the
corner candy store than mine did, but Marty was only rarely
to be seen hanging out in the back booths or standing outside
by the fire hydrant where I would sometimes amuse the corner regulars with takeoffs of the school principal and the local
rabbi.

Marty attended a small college of about 1,900 students
whose name meant as little to me as Wake Forest or Bowling
Green—Bucknell University, in Lewisburg, Pennsylvania. It
wasn't what he said about his studies that made me want to
find out more but that he appeared to have absorbed there
precisely the qualities that he'd been devoid of as an adolescent, the sort of poise and savoir faire that encouraged a boy
to run for student-council president or to date the most popular girl in class. In only a matter of weeks this kid, whom I
had thought of as being in the shadow of more intense, lo-

quacious types like me, had developed a confident, outgoing manner that smacked of maturity. There was even a girlfriend, whom he spoke of without a trace of his old shyness. I was astonished: I was still on Leslie Street, keeping my father at bay by heeding high school rules of conduct, while Marty appeared to have entered adult society.

I couldn't forget what he'd said about the girl: he would pick her up at her dormitory in the morning and they'd walk to class together across the campus. It wasn't the romantic idyll that impressed me so much as the matter-of-factness. At this college called Bucknell, in less than a semester, Marty Castlebaum had become an independent young man sounding an independent young man's prerogatives without shame or guilt or secrecy. At Newark Rutgers, I might be becoming more of a Newarker and an American but I couldn't fool myself, even with the pipe and the Trojans, about feeling more like a man.

IN MARCH OF 1951 my parents and I made the seven-hour drive to Lewisburg, about sixty miles up from Harrisburg, in a farming valley along the Susquehanna River; it was a town of about five thousand people, situated at the heart of one of the most conservative Republican counties in the state. I was to be interviewed by an assistant to the director of admissions, a courteous middle-aged woman whose name I've by now forgotten. In her office Miss Blake, let's call her, told the three of us that with my high school standing and my Newark Rutgers grades I'd have no trouble being admitted with full credit for my freshman courses. She was less optimistic about my receiving financial aid as a transfer student but assured us that I'd be in a better position to compete for a scholarship after having proved myself at Bucknell.

I was upset to hear that; part of the problem, I figured, had to do with my father's promotion. Even though a big chunk of his salary still went to paying off his business debt, his earnings had increased measurably since he'd taken over as manager of the Union City office, and there had been no choice but to give the correct figure on my aid-application form. Yet, for reasons of pride and privacy, he forbade me to report the debt. To make matters worse, we didn't look like a family in need. If anything, my mother, in a demure navy-blue dress, was dressed more attractively—though with no less propriety—than the assistant to the director of admissions; for jewelry she wore the little gold pin she'd been awarded after serving two terms as president of the PTA. She was forty-seven then, a slender, attractive woman with graying dark hair and lively brown eyes whose appearance and comportment were thoroughly Americanized. In fact, she was never wholly at ease except among Jews and for that reason cherished our part of Newark. She kept a kosher kitchen, lit Sabbath candles, and happily fulfilled all the Passover dietary regulations, though less out of religious proclivity than because of deep ties to her childhood household and to her mother, whose ideas of what made for a properly run Jewish home she wished to satisfy and uphold; being a Jew among Jews was, simply, one of her deepest pleasures. In a predominantly gentile environment, however, she lost her social suppleness and something too of her confidence, and her instinctive respectability came to seem more of a shield with which to safeguard herself than the natural expression of her decency.

But this self-consciousness should not be exaggerated; I'm sure that to Miss Blake, during my Bucknell interview, my mother seemed nothing more or less than perfectly agreeable and ladylike.

My father, a fit and solid-looking man of fifty, with thinning hair and rimless spectacles, wore a dark business suit with a vest and looked like someone who himself sat behind a desk and interviewed applicants, as indeed he frequently had done while reorganizing the unproductive staff at the Union City office. He certainly was not uneasy being inside a university building for the first time. The turnabout in his fortunes (and ours) had renewed his prodigious energies; between that and his almost palpable pride in me and my scholastic success, he radiated an unpolished, good-natured confidence that stirred my own pride but that, I felt certain, was killing my chances for a Bucknell scholarship. Had he been an embarrassment (and of course beforehand I feared he might be), had he tried too hard, setting out to sell Bucknell on what a good boy I was or telling Miss Blake about the progress made in America by our vast array of relatives, we could, in fact, have been in better shape for seeming that much cruder. As it was, the picture we presented, of a self-made, enterprising, happily cohesive and prospering family, convinced me that I was doomed. I'd get into Bucknell, all right, but for lack of funds I wouldn't be able to enroll.

Later that day Marty Castlebaum took us on a tour of the university grounds and around the charming tree-lined streets leading to the main shopping thoroughfare, where we had rooms for the night in the Hotel Lewisburger. Not since I'd been to Princeton with my Uncle Ed had I strolled around a town where people actually lived in houses dating back to the eighteenth century. On a tiny green near his fraternity house there was a Civil War cannon that Marty daringly told my parents went off "when a virgin walks by."

It was the campus that most beguiled me: ivy-covered brick buildings sparsely set amid large trees and long, rolling lawns. On "the Hill," at the heart of the campus, the windows of the

men's dormitory looked beyond cornfields and pastures to the
Lycoming hills. There was a clock in the cupola of the men's
dorm that chimed on the hour, an elegant spire atop the new
library, a student hangout that Marty familiarly called Chet's
(though a sign identified it as The Bison), and a dormitory
called Larison Hall, where that girlfriend of his had her room.
Scattered about the campus and on streets down from the
Hill were a dozen or so manorial-looking buildings with fa-
cades inspired either by English stately homes or by colon-
naded plantation dwellings; here lived the fraternity men. In
all, it was an unoutlandish little college town of the kind I'd
seen before only in movies with Kay Kyser or June Allyson,
not so much subdued or genteel, and certainly not posh or
gentrified, but instead suited for the coziest, most common-
place dreams of order. Lewisburg emanated an unpretentious
civility that we could trust, rather than an air of privilege by
which we might have been intimidated. To be sure, everything about the rural landscape and the small-town setting
(and Miss Blake) suggested an unmistakably gentile version
of unpretentious civility, but by 1951 none of us thought it
pretentious or unseemly that the momentum of our family's
Americanization should have carried us, in half a century,
from my Yiddish-speaking grandparents' hard existence in
Newark's poorest ghetto neighborhood to this pretty place
whose harmonious nativeness was proclaimed in every view.

My parents turned out to have been as impressed as I was,
though probably less by Bucknell's collegiate look than by our
enthusiastic guide, a Jewish boy from our block who seemed
to them, as he did to me, to be thriving wonderfully in this
unfamiliar atmosphere. After dinner in the hotel restaurant,
when Marty had left for his dormitory and we were in the
elevator on our way up to bed, my father said to me, "You
like it, don't you?" "Yes, but how can we afford it if they won't

give me a scholarship for September?" "Forget the scholarship," he told me. "You want to go here, you're going."

I sat up late at the little desk in my room, a stack of hotel stationery at the ready for recording my "thoughts." I replayed over and over the conversation with my father in the hotel elevator, adding a line of my own that I would not have had the self-control to say to him face-to-face but that I was able to write freely and exuberantly on a sheet of the Lewisburger's paper. I felt a buoyant sense of having survived the worst while preserving unimpaired the long-standing preuniversity accord that would seem to have made us an indestructible family: "And now we won't have to have that terrible fight—we've been saved by Bucknell."

Over precisely the issue that had been simmering since I'd begun college—my weekend whereabouts after midnight—my father and I did, of course, have the terrible fight, when I was home from Lewisburg for my first midyear vacation. And it was worse than I had foreseen, however banal the immediate cause. Along with my mother, my brother—who fortunately happened to be in from Manhattan, where he was beginning to establish himself as a commercial artist—made every conceivable effort to act as a peacemaker and, with an air of urgent diplomacy, hurried back and forth between the two ends of the apartment, where the two raving belligerents were isolated. And though, after two days of histrionic shouting and bitter silence, my father and I—for the sake, finally, of my desolated mother—negotiated a fragile truce, I returned to Bucknell a shell-shocked son, freshly evacuated from the Oedipal battlefield, in dire need of rest and rehabilitation.

AN ATTRACTIVE WHITE Christian male entering Bucknell in the early fifties could expect to be officially courted by about half the thirteen fraternities. A promising athlete, the graduate of a prestigious prep school, the son of rich parents or of a distinguished alumnus, might wind up with bids from as many as ten fraternities. A Jewish freshman—or Jewish transfer student, like me—could expect to be rushed by two fraternities at most, the exclusively Jewish fraternity, Sigma Alpha Mu, which, like the Christian fraternities, was the local chapter of a national body, and Phi Lambda Theta, a local fraternity without national affiliations, which did not discriminate on the basis of race, religion, or color. A Jewish student who wished to take part in fraternity life but was acceptable to neither was in trouble. If he couldn't bear being an "independent"—taking meals in the university dining hall, living in the dormitories or in a room in town, making friends and dating outside the reigning social constellation—he'd have to pack up and go home. There were a few reported cases of Jewish students who had.

The Jewish fraternity had nothing much that was Jewish about it except the wholly sanctioned nickname by which the members were identified, at Bucknell and at every other campus where there was a chapter of Sigma Alpha Mu: as easily by themselves as by others, the Jewish brothers were called Sammies. Had the fraternity been christened Iota Kappa Epsilon, people might not have tolerated Ikeys so readily, but no one seemed to have ever considered Sammies an even mildly stigmatizing label. Perhaps its purpose was prophylactic, preempting the attribution of diminutives less benign than this friendly-sounding acronym, which carried in its suffix only the tiniest sting. I, for one, never became accustomed to hearing it and never could say it, but probably I had been sensitized unduly by Budd Schulberg's novel, which I'd read in high school, about the pushiest of pushy Jews, Sammy Glick.

Certainly the Sammy kitchen, where three meals a day were prepared for the sixty-five or so members, smelled more like the galley of a merchant ship than like the sanctum sanctorum of a traditional Jewish household. "Cookie," the chef, was a local Navy veteran, a grim-faced, tattooed little man with a loose lantern jaw bearing a day or two's dark stubble; he wouldn't have been out of place frying onions on the grill of a back-road diner anywhere in America. Eggs with ham or bacon was the staple for breakfast, and pork chops and ham steaks showed up for lunch or dinner a couple of times a week—fare no different from what was served in the other fraternity houses and at the student dining hall. But you didn't join the Jewish fraternity to eat kosher food any more than to observe the Sabbath, to study Torah, or to discuss Jewish questions of the day; nor did you join because you hoped to rid yourself of embarrassing Jewish ways. Most likely you came from a family, like my own, for whom assimilation wasn't a potent issue any longer—if it had been, you wouldn't have come to Bucknell to begin with or have remained very long. This isn't to say that their Jewish parents would have preferred a university decree that these Sammy sons be allowed to join the otherwise Christian-dominated fraternities. No, in 1951 Sigma Alpha Mu suited everybody. The Jews were together because they were profoundly different but otherwise like everyone else.

As it happened, an opportunity to be the only Jew to pledge a gentile fraternity was offered to me when I arrived, as a sophomore, in September of 1951. I was rushed not only by the Jewish Sigma Alpha Mu and the nondenominational Phi Lambda Theta but also by Theta Chi. For reasons never entirely explained to me, Theta Chi had among its sixty-odd gentile members one Jew already, a senior with a gentile name and un-Jewish appearance who was also the fraternity president and who worked hard to entice me into the house, though my own name and appearance weren't likely to fool anyone. I took the invitation seriously and during the rushing period ate there as a guest several times. If I was joining a fraternity— and I figured that penetrating student society as a sophomore outside a fraternity might be nearly impossible—then didn't it make sense for me, with my democratic ideals and liberal principles, to capitalize on this inexplicable breach in a tightly segregated system?

Membership in Theta Chi certainly sounded more adventurous to a boy from the Weequahic section of Newark than slipping predictably in with the Jews. As for the nondenominational fraternity, whose unpretentious house on a back street was home to nearly a hundred young men, it seemed to me, after a quick appraisal, that the members I met were either innocently upright in their devotion to their principles or shy and socially a bit uncertain, boys who could indeed not have had anywhere else to go. I might have had this wrong, but I was struck by an air of charity and virtue about the place that was more purely "Christian" than anything I'd run into in a nominally Christian but essentially areligious fraternity like Theta Chi—something smacking a little of the goodness of the Salvation Army. Everything else aside, I believed I would need a slightly more profligate, less utopian atmosphere in which to realize even a tenth of the nefarious erotic prospectus that—as my father correctly surmised—I had been secretly preparing for years. The estimable goals of the Phi Lambda Thetas made the house too much like home.

At all costs my choice had to have nothing to do with my parents' preference, since establishing my independence was the point of coming away. In a series of letters home I laid out the problem in a scrupulously maniacal presentation worthy of Kafka. Instead of replying instinctively to what must have sounded to them like so much foolish naïveté, they were sufficiently intimidated by all my pages to seek out the advice of the Greens, Jewish friends in the clothing business whose daughter had manifested a similar urge a few years earlier. The line they took over the phone wasn't without wisdom: they said they wanted me to do what would make me "happiest." If I thought I would be happier with boys whose backgrounds were unlike my own, then I should of course choose Theta Chi; but if in the end it seemed as evident to me as to them and to the Greens that I would be happier with boys like Marty Castlebaum, whose backgrounds resembled mine, then I should choose SAM. *They* would be happy, my mother told me—it was she, whose touch was lighter, who'd been assigned to speak for their side—with whatever choice was sure to make *me* happy . . . and so on.

Had I joined Theta Chi as their new Jew, the chances are that challenging convention might well have proved invigorating for a while and that discovering the secrets of this unknown community would, at the start, have yielded some genuine anthropological excitement. It probably wouldn't have been long, however, before I found the exuberant side of my personality, the street-corner taste for comic mockery and for ludicrous, theatrical speculation, out of place in the Theta Chi dining room with its staid, prosaic, small-town decorum that had struck me as somewhat cornball. Probably my career as a Theta Chi would have been even shorter than my career as a Sammy was to be. I wasn't afraid of the temptation to become an honorary WASP but was leery of a communal spirit that might lead me to self-censorship, since the last thing I'd left home for was to become encased in somebody else's idea of what I should be. Eventually I came round to understanding that joining Theta Chi could wind up being a far more conformist act than taking the seemingly conventional course of being with boys from backgrounds more like my own, who, just *because* their style was familiar, wouldn't have the power to inhibit my expressive yearnings. Coming from backgrounds like mine, a few of them might have similar yearnings themselves.

A few did—two, to be precise, both sophomore English majors: Pete Tasch, from Baltimore, and Dick Minton, from Mount Vernon, New York. Pete, who later became an English professor, was a very highly tuned boy with a strong strain of bookish refinement that set him apart not only from the regular fellows at the fraternity but even more blatantly from the kids calling to him for their Cokes and fries at the Sweet Shop, a local hangout where he clocked afternoon and evening hours in order to pay his living expenses. Dick, who eventually became a lawyer, was more unshakable, a straight shooter wholly without airs and with a very good brain, who listened to Beethoven quartets whenever he wasn't reading. His intense cultural passions could have been shared by no more than a dozen students on the campus and by hardly anyone at the fraternity house. In the winter of 1952, a little over a year after I'd enrolled at Bucknell, we three resigned from Sigma Alpha Mu and gave our devotion instead to *Et Cetera*, a literary magazine that we'd helped to found and then took over, under my editorship in 1952–53 and the next year under Pete's, with Dick as literary editor.

The fraternity divided pretty much into two groups: the commerce-and-finance majors preparing for business careers or law school and those in the sciences aiming for medical school; there were a couple of engineers and, aside from us three, only a handful of liberal-arts students. Before emerging literary interests forged my alliance with Pete Tasch and Dick Minton, the Sammy whose company I'd most enjoyed was a C&F student, Dick Denholtz, a burly, assertive, dark-bearded boy whose jovial forcefulness I associated with those peculiarly Jewish energies that gave my Newark neighborhood its distinctive exuberance. Dick came from the Newark suburbs, and perhaps what accounted for our strong, short-lived affinity was that his family's American roots were like my own in urban Jewish New Jersey. Together we could be the coarse and uninhibited performers who ignited whatever improvisational satire flared up in the living room after dinner; the Sammy musical skit for the interfraternity Mid-Term Jubilee—a telescoped version of *Guys and Dolls* improbably set at Bucknell—had been written and directed by Dick Denholtz and me and starred the two of us in raucous singing roles. Our spirited low-comedy concoctions—the kind that I had thought unlikely to find a responsive audience at the Theta Chi house—constituted SAM's single, unmistakable strain of "Jewishness": in the ways that the extroverts made fun of things, and the ways that the others found us funny, Sigma Alpha Mu came closest, in my estimation, to being a Jewish fraternity.

I never knew how the predominantly Protestant student body perceived the Jewish fraternity. Almost two-thirds of Bucknell's students were from small towns in Pennsylvania and New Jersey, while the preponderance of Sammies came from New York—most of them from Westchester County and Long Island, a few from the city itself. Of course there must have been coeds whose families preferred that they not date Jews and who willingly obeyed, but as there were barely twenty Jewish women on the campus, and about eighty Jewish men, the dates I saw at Sammy parties were mostly gentiles, many from communities where there were probably no Jews at all. Over the years Sigma Alpha Mu had staunchly sought, and frequently won, the interfraternity academic trophy, and though there weren't enough Sammies playing on varsity teams to give the house an athletic aura (in my time just two basketball players and two football players), the sensational *social* event of the early fifties was our brainchild. The nature of the event suggests (as did the brazen Jubilee *Guys and Dolls*) that going along like sensible assimilationists with traditional campus socializing conventions was not the primary motive of the Sammies' leadership. The aim was to make a mark as a distinctively uninhibited, freewheeling fraternity.

The idea for the "Sand Blast" was not original to our chapter but borrowed from a fraternity at some larger university like Syracuse or Cornell, where the motif of an indoor winter beach party was supposed to have inspired a colossal success of just the sort the Bucknell Sammies hoped would elevate them to the forefront of campus popularity. The rugs and the furniture, the trophy cabinets and the pictures on the walls, were all to be removed from the downstairs rooms, and the first floor of the house—dining hall and two living rooms— was to be covered with about three inches of sand and planted with beach umbrellas. The floor would have to be braced from below to bear the weight of the sand; what's more, after the sand dumped inside proved uninvitingly clammy, it had to be heated with strong lights in order to reduce the dampness, which had dangerously increased the weight of the load. Required dress was a bathing suit (in March), and the entire student body was invited. To spread the word, signs were posted all over the campus, and one afternoon a small plane flew low over the campus issuing the invitation through a loudspeaker.

During the planning stages I expressed uneasiness with the expense and the vastness of the effort and with what seemed a clownish misuse of the physical structure itself; though by no means an architectural showpiece, the building possessed its own lumpish, sturdy 1920s integrity and served, after all, as our collective home. I assured the brothers that I was as delighted as anyone by the prospect of producing this pornographic tableau within our familiar walls, and of course charmed by the idea of all those Bucknell coeds lying around on the sand in their two-piece swimsuits, openly contravening the strict dress code enforced by the Honor Council (a group of esteemed women students who tried infractions of conduct among their peers and handed out punishment when a coed was found, say, to be walking on a college path in a pair of Bermuda shorts half an inch shorter than prescribed). I was no enemy of the flesh, I said, but I reminded my brothers that when the party was over and our house, if it was still standing, had again become a home, we would be chewing sand in our mashed potatoes for semesters to come. I was roundly shouted down.

Among those few who argued that the plans for the Sand Blast were too grandiosely whatever—childish, ostentatious, imprudent, crazy—Tasch, Minton, and I were the least enamored of all; we were by then trying to put out four issues a year of a new magazine, inspired by Addison, Steele, and Harold Ross, and felt ourselves being swallowed up like extras in a show-biz production by Mike Todd.

Despite throngs of students who dropped their coats and shoes and scarves into a vast pile in the basement and then came upstairs to disperse themselves, nearly nude, across the indoor beach, the Sand Blast came off without a cave-in or an invasion by the university police. Had there been a chance of anything like an orgy developing, ninety percent (more!) of those who had showed up would have left for The Spit (as the crummy local movie house was known on campus) without even the intervention of the authorities, and I, along with my date from Chester, Pennsylvania, would probably have gone with them. Fantasy was of course less bridled than if the girls had arrived corsaged and swathed in taffeta, as they customarily did for a fraternity's annual lavish party, but in the fifties Bucknell, with its freshman hazing and its compulsory chapel, its pinning ceremonies and heralded "Hello Spirit," was still a long way from Berkeley, 1968, and Woodstock, 1970, let alone from the hanging gardens of Plato's Retreat.

The strain of Dadaesque Jewish showmanship that manifested itself a decade later in cultural-political deviants and cunningly anarchic entrepreneurs—mischief-makers as diverse as Jerry Rubin and Abbie Hoffman, the Chicago Seven defendants; William Kunstler, the Chicago Seven lawyer; Tuli Kupferberg, the Fug poet and a leading contributor to *Fuck You/A Magazine of the Arts*; Hillard Elkins, the producer of *Oh, Calcutta!*; Al Goldstein, the publisher of *Screw*; not to mention Allen Ginsberg, Bella Abzug, Lenny Bruce, Norman Mailer, and me—was hardly what was germinating at the Sammy Sand Blast. Though a spark of defiant impudence had perhaps ignited the first fraternity meeting where so outlandish an idea was considered seriously, the stunt was engineered finally by conventional, law-abiding fraternity boys in training for secure careers in orderly middle-class American communities. The Sand Blast's underlying erotic motive may have spilled out more playfully, with more imaginative flair, than what fired the campus panty raid later that year, but what prevailed was the poolside spirit of the suburban country club.

Actually, the mob of freshman and sophomore men that came surging off the Hill one April night—hoping to break in on the nightgowned coeds and steal their underwear—produced a far more orgiastic version than the Sammies had of a Sadean scenario. The exhibitionistic extravaganza plotted and bankrolled by the socially competitive Sammies, though as bold a challenge to standards of communal decency as any mounted in Lewisburg during my years there, had, in fact, less to do with the suppressed longings that would culminate in the sexual uprising of the sixties than did the rowdy testicularity of those spontaneous spring panty raids that seemed meaningless to me at the time.

"LET'S START A MAGAZINE . . . fearlessly obscene. . . ." The mockingly inspirational line was from E. E. Cummings, whose poetry I'd begun reading (and reciting to friends) under the influence of Robert Maurer, a young American-literature instructor in the English department, who was doing a Ph.D. dissertation on Cummings and whose wife, Charlotte, had been William Shawn's secretary at the *New Yorker* before marrying Bob and arriving with him in Lewisburg. With an M.A. from Montclair State College and his incomplete Wisconsin Ph.D., Bob was probably being paid about half as much as my father had earned struggling to support us on an insurance agent's salary, and one of the first things that I came to admire about the Maurers was their pennilessness; it seemed to confer an admirable independence from convention without having turned them, tiresomely, into fifties bohemians. Our bohemian—or the closest you came to one in Lewisburg—was the artist-in-residence Bruce Mitchell, who taught painting classes, loved bop, drank some, and had a wife who wore long peasant skirts. The Maurers seemed to me free (in the biggest and best sense), levelheaded Americans, respectable enough but unconcerned with position and appearances. They had their books and records, their old car, and a little brick house rather bare of furniture; Bob's droopy old jacket was patched at the elbows for other than ornamental reasons—yet what they didn't own they didn't appear to miss. They made being poor look so easy that I decided to follow their example and become poor myself someday, either as an

English professor like Bob or as a serious writer who was so good that his books made no money. Bob, a butcher's son, was very much a Depression-honed city boy, originally from my part of industrial New Jersey. He was so lanky and small-headed, however, that in his oval spectacles and fraying clothes he looked more like an educated hayseed, some string-bean farm boy who had struggled semiconsciously toward freedom in a Sherwood Anderson novel. His direct manner, too, seemed to be born of the open spaces, and some twenty years later, after he had got fed up with teaching and had quit his professorship at Antioch, he earned his living writing for *Current Biography* and *Field and Stream*. He wound up, all on his own and seemingly quite happy, coaching boys' baseball for the Peace Corps in the wilds of Chile. He died of a heart attack in 1983, at the age of sixty-two. At his funeral his son, Harry, who'd been born in Lewisburg while I was a student there, read aloud from Bob's favorite Hemingway story, "Big Two-Hearted River."

Charlotte had her own brand of unadorned down-to-earthness, which filtered attractively through a faint Florida accent; she was psychologically more delicate than Bob and from a slightly more prosperous background, and to me her unorthodox Antioch College education and her time at the *New Yorker* made her seem terrifically urbane. She had a prognathous, fresh kind of freckled good looks that was as appealing as her speech, but it wasn't until I'd graduated from college and spent a week with the Maurers in their primitive cabin on the bluff of a tiny Maine island that I allowed myself, on the walks we took together, to fall for my professor's wife. At eighteen I was thrilled enough just to have been befriended by them and to be asked to their house occasionally on Saturday nights to hear their E. E. Cummings record and drink their Gallo wine or to listen to Bob talk about growing up gentile in the working-class town of Roselle, New Jersey, during the twenties and thirties.

I talked freely to them about my own upbringing, a twenty-minute drive from Bob's old family house in Roselle, which bordered on Elizabeth, where my mother's immigrant parents had settled separately, as young people, at the start of the century. Along with Jack and Joan Wheatcroft, another young English-department couple who soon became confidants and close friends, the Maurers must have been the first gentiles to whom I'd ever given an insider's view of my Jewish neighborhood, my family, and our friends. When I jumped up from the table to mimic my more colorful relations, I found they were not merely entertained but interested, and they encouraged me to tell more about where I was from. Nonetheless, so long as I was earnestly reading my way from Cynewulf to *Mrs. Dalloway*—and so long as I was enrolled at a college where the five percent of Jewish students left no mark on the prevailing undergraduate style—it did not dawn on me that these anecdotes and observations might be made into literature, however fictionalized they'd already become in the telling. Thomas Wolfe's exploitation of Asheville or Joyce's of Dublin suggested nothing about focusing this urge to write on my own experience. How could Art be rooted in a parochial Jewish Newark neighborhood having nothing to do with the enigma of time and space or good and evil or appearance and reality?

The imitations with which I entertained the Maurers and the Wheatcrofts were of somebody's shady uncle the bookie and somebody's sharpie son the street-corner bongo player and of the comics Stinky and Shorty, whose routines I'd learned at the Empire Burlesque in downtown Newark. The stories I told them were about the illicit love life of our cocky, self-important neighbor the tiny immigrant Seltzer King and

the amazing appetite—for jokes, pickles, pinochle, everything—of our family friend the 300-pound bon vivant Apple
King, while the stories I *wrote*, set absolutely nowhere, were
mournful little things about sensitive children, sensitive adolescents, and sensitive young men crushed by coarse life.
The stories were intended to be "touching"; without entirely
knowing it, I wanted through my fiction to become "refined,"
to be elevated into realms unknown to the lower-middle-class
Jews of Leslie Street, with their focus on earning a living and
raising a family and trying occasionally to have a good time.
To prove in my earliest undergraduate stories that I was a
nice Jewish boy would have been bad enough; this was
worse—proving that I was a nice boy, period. The Jew was
nowhere to be seen; there were no Jews in the stories, no
Newark, and not a sign of comedy—the last thing I wanted
to do was to hand anybody a laugh in literature. I wanted to
show that life was sad and poignant, even while I was expe-
riencing it as heady and exhilarating; I wanted to demonstrate
that I was "compassionate," a totally harmless person.

In those first undergraduate stories I managed to extract
from Salinger a very cloying come-on and from the young
Capote his gossamer vulnerability, and to imitate badly my
titan, Thomas Wolfe, at the extremes of self-pitying self-
importance. Those stories were as naïve as a student's can
be, and I was only lucky that I was on a campus like Bucknell where there wasn't an intellectual faction to oppose my
minute coterie, for its members would have found in my
fiction a very soft satiric target. Then again, if there had
been some sort of worthy competition around, I might not
have produced these unconscious personal allegories to begin
with. Allegorical representation is what they were—the result
of having found myself far more of a cuckoo in the Bucknell
nest than I'd been even as an adolescent on Leslie Street, let

alone at Newark Rutgers, where, as a lower-middle-class boy from an ambitious minority in pursuit of a better life, I'd briefly played out the postimmigrant romance of higher education.

I don't believe I ever found myself out of place just because I was a Jew, though I was not unaware, especially when I was still fresh from home, that I *was* a Jew at a university where the bylaws stipulated that more than half the Board of Trustees had to be members of the Baptist Church, where chapel attendance was required of lowerclassmen, and where the one extracurricular organization for which most Bucknellians seemed to have membership cards was the Christian Association. But then, after only a little while in SAM I felt no closer to my fraternity brothers than I had to those Christian Association members who had lived in my dormitory and spent a part of each evening playing touch football in the corridor outside the room where I was concocting the symbols for my stories of victimized refinement. Like the overprotected young victims in those first short stories, who stood for something like the life of the mind, I was turning out to be too sensitive, though not to religious so much as to spiritual differences at a university where the dominant tone seemed to emanate from the large undergraduate population enrolled in the commerce-and-finance program—students preparing to take ordinary workaday jobs in the booming postwar business world, which not only my literary ideals but also my loosely held suspicion of the profit motive had pitted me against since I'd begun to read the New York paper *P.M.*, when I was fourteen. The courses to which I was drawn typified everything that the marketplace deemed worthless, and yet here I was, living among its most enthusiastic adherents— the unrebellious sons and daughters of status-quo America at the dawn of the Eisenhower era—certain that mind and not money was what gave life meaning, and studying, in dead earnest, Literary Criticism, Modern Thought, Advanced Shakespeare, and Aesthetics.

In September of 1952, when, as juniors, I took over as editor in chief of *Et Cetera* and Pete Tasch as managing editor, the Maurers became our advisers. Bob was listed as an official literary adviser, and Charlotte became an unofficial adviser. Her influence on the opening pages of each issue would have been apparent to anyone familiar with the *New Yorker*'s "Talk of the Town." Our own "Talk of the Town" was a two-page miscellany of putatively witty reportage, called "Transit Lines," a heading we thought nicely appropriate on a campus where an engineering student was always out on one of the walkways sighting through a telescope. Stories began in the first person plural, invariably with a tone of droll breeziness that the editor considered urbane: "When we heard about the new dormitory inspection policy (men living on The Hill will have their rooms inspected every week by the ROTC department) we were prepared to see, lining the campus, signs screaming, 'Down with the Military' or 'Keep the Fascista from Our Rooms! . . .'" "The other day we purchased a genuine undyed mouton pelt for the ridiculously low sum of five dollars. . . ." "One of our friends, a sociology major, if you're interested, told us a story the other afternoon. It seems that he took the afternoon train out of New York on Sunday. . . ." Some pieces were deft and readable, others oozed with archness, and none accorded with Cummings's prescription for a magazine "fearlessly obscene."

The obscenity around, in "our" judgment, was the weekly student newspaper, the *Bucknellian*, to which *Et Cetera* hoped to propose a sophisticated alternative. Little more than a decade later, student dissidents would display their defiance of officially sanctioned campus values by promoting, in their publications, bad taste and outlaw behavior; in the early fifties those of us keen to exhibit our superior wit and offhand charm in these "Transit Lines" pieces were indeed the Bucknell dissidents, and yet it was purportedly to raise, not to drag down, the tone of the place that we struck our *New Yorker*ish poses. Realistically, nobody working for the magazine expected it to do anything other than make tangible the differences between the collective student sensibility and our own as it was quickly altering under the influence of the English professors whose favorites we were and who were teaching us to enjoy using a word like "sensibility." But to me, at least, these differences seemed to reflect the national division between the civilized minority who had voted for Adlai Stevenson and the philistine majority who had overwhelmingly elected Eisenhower President.

The day after Stevenson was beaten, I stood up in Professor Harry Garvin's English 257 (Shakespeare: Intensive study of a small number of plays) and, under the pretext of explicating a passage about the mob in *Coriolanus*, excoriated the American public (and, by implication, the Bucknell student body, which had solidly favored Eisenhower) for having chosen a war hero over an intellectual statesman. Even though his gaze suggested that I was wildly out of order, Garvin, perhaps because of his own similar disappointment, let me go on to the end uninterrupted, while a majority of the Shakespeare students registered either amusement or boredom with my tirade. Absolutely certain that I was right and that a moronic America was our fate, I sat down thinking that despite the very obvious classroom consensus, *they* were the ones who were the dangerous fools.

This outburst aside, it had never occurred to me to make a case for Stevenson on the editorial page of *Et Cetera* when my first issue appeared at the height of the presidential campaign in October of 1952. The magazine had "higher" purposes, *literary* purposes; besides, it was not the custom in those days for student publications to support candidates for public office. A year later the magazine did publish a page-long "prose poem" that I'd written over the summer vacation, a monologue by an unnamed coward too prudent to speak out against McCarthyism, which provoked no response at all, so it may well have been that an *Et Cetera* editorial supporting Stevenson wouldn't have bothered anyone. But at the time, had I even thought of writing one, I would have assumed that it would violate the policy of the university Board of Publications, with which I was soon to collide anyway. I sported a Stevenson button in Republican Lewisburg and later, during the McCarthy hearings, I would come down off the Hill to the Maurer house at lunchtime and, according to a recollection of Charlotte Maurer's, stalk up and down the living room, glowering, while Bob and I listened to the proceedings on the radio. That was as far, however, as my political activism went.

The cadences of the editorial that I did publish in October 1952 bespeak, alas, the influence of the "March of Time" on my polemical style; in retrospect the editorial looks a little like the budding of an incipient Kennedy speech writer, concluding as it does with the line "Let our generation not wait too long." Written as an elegiac plea to my contemporaries to abandon their "high school values," their "football-clothes-car-date-acne-conscious brains," it was, in fact, a covertly condescending, less simpering version of my allegories about displacement. The editorial made the case, however naïvely, for a kind of robust, responsible maturity that was an advance over the prissy tenderness with which the author of the fiction had chosen to associate his manliness.

The editorial of the midyear issue was tame and informative and meant to be charming—a history, beginning in 1870, of the rise and fall of the Bucknell literary magazines that pre-

ceded *Et Cetera*. A laconic last paragraph quoted "Scott Fitzgerald." "What is it Scott Fitzgerald said? 'So we beat on,
boats against the current, borne back ceaselessly into the
past.' " The third issue, out in the spring of 1953, when I had
just turned twenty, made me notorious, or as notorious as one
could be who wore dirty white bucks and was on the dean's
list; it defined me (perhaps in my own mind, primarily) as the
college's critical antagonist rather than a boy who secretly still
possessed enough of his own "high school values" to want to
be popular and admired. Since the *Bucknellian* exemplified
for me and my *Et Cetera* friends the lowbrow campus enthusiasms by which we felt engulfed, I put aside the self-
protective writing postures with which I had kept my sense
of estrangement in check and launched a heavily sarcastic
attack on the banality of the weekly paper and its editor,
Barbara Roemer, a well-liked, very amiable young woman
from Springfield, New Jersey, who was the vice-president of
the Tri Delt sorority and the captain of the cheerleading
squad. As it was only the year before—while still a Sammy
with a social identity outside the literary clique—that I'd un-
successfully dated two pretty, clean-cut girls with ordinary
American names wholly exotic to my ear, *both* of them members of the cheerleading squad, the reader is free to wonder
how much of the animus directed against Barbara Roemer
might have been inspired by my failure to impress either
Annette Littlefield or Pat McColl.

"There is a theory," began the barrage, "that if a thousand
monkeys were chained to a thousand typewriters for an un-
specified number of years, they would have written all of the
great literature that has been set down in the world by human
beings. If such is the case, what is holding up production on
the *Bucknellian*? We do not expect Miss Roemer and her
cohorts to turn out great literature, for, after all, they are not

monkeys, but we do expect them to publish a newspaper."
The centerfold of the magazine was a satiric send-up of the
newspaper, a facsimile front page burlesquing the *Bucknellian's* editorial column and its newsless news stories, the work
of someone seemingly more subtly endowed with aggressive
skills than the insulting, ungrammatical editor in chief of *Et
Cetera*. Without thinking too much about it, I had extracted
from my taste for mimicry a rhetorical disguise more stylishly
combative than the adolescent penchant for righteous contempt; transforming indignation into performance, I managed
on the facsimile front page to reveal a flash of talent for comic
destruction.

For delivering this gleeful one-two punch to an innocuous
Bucknell institution, I was admonished by the dean of men,
Mal Musser, and brought before the Board of Publications
for censure. In addition, the managing editor of the paper,
Red Macauley, knocked on the door of my dormitory room
and, with his fists clenched at his sides, told me that somebody
ought to give me what I deserved for what I had done to
Bobby Roemer. Our argument in the doorway was heated,
but as Macauley was acting, by and large, out of chivalry and
in fact had no more of a taste for physical combat than I did,
he never took the swing that my adrenaline was readying me
for. Dean Musser talked to me about the meaning of the word
"tradition" and invoked the "Bucknell spirit," but as I had
already heard him express himself on these subjects on nu-
merous public occasions, I came away from that dressing-
down feeling more or less unharmed. My appearance before
the student-faculty Board of Publications must have been far
more trying, for, as it happens, I don't remember it at all and
was only recently reminded that it took place by my former
teacher Mildred Martin, whose writing tutorial I was taking
that semester and whose senior honors seminar, later, was

the backbone of my undergraduate education. At my request, some months back, Mildred—who is now eighty-three—sent me entries from her 1953–54 journals about the senior seminar and appended some random notes under the title "Memories." One note reads: "After Roth was called up for reprimand because of an *Etc*. issue satirizing the *Bucknellian*, he came in distress to see me. I told him that any satirist in America would be subject to criticism." I called Mildred, in Lewisburg, after reading this and told her that thirty-four years later, in my Connecticut studio, I had no recollection of the reprimand from the Board of Publications or of rushing off afterward to be consoled by her. "Oh, yes," she told me over the phone, "when you came to my house you were nearly in tears."

THE DECALS I'D AFFIXED to the rear window of my father's Chevy during the first vacation of my sophomore year—one proclaiming the name of my new university, the other the Greek initials of my fraternity—I scraped off with a razor blade a year later. My sardonic uncle the dry cleaner, who, when he'd seen the decals, had taken to calling me "Joe College," didn't seem to notice when they were gone, and to him I remained Joe College until I came out of the Army, in 1956, and got a job teaching freshman composition at the University of Chicago. From then on I was "The Professor." But the professor had already begun to emerge by the time I returned as a twenty-year-old to begin my senior year, in September 1953. I had by then passed beyond the eventful semesters defining myself as the outspoken enemy of what seemed pleasantly acceptable to nearly everyone else, and had become a zealous student in The Seminar. This was the elite two-semester honors course, carrying a total of eighteen credit hours, presided over by Mildred Martin—"independent read-

ing in English literature, from its beginnings to the present."
The reading list was ambitious—at least a couple of books a
week, plus fifty pages of details to master in Baugh's *Literary
History of England*. There was also a long critical essay due
weekly, and every word, spoken in class or written, was scru-
tinized for accuracy and for common sense by Miss Martin,
a plainspoken, businesslike Midwesterner with short gray hair
and rimless spectacles, whose crisp laugh and uncarping nature, along with her solid learning, made her exactly the humane intellectual disciplinarian I was ripe for. There were
eight in the seminar at its peak, four men and four women,
but discussion tended to be dominated, sometimes auda-
ciously, by the *Et Cetera* editorial staff—Pete Tasch, Dick
Minton, and me.

That fall the seminar assembled from 1:30 to 4:30 every
Thursday afternoon in the living room of the house on South
Front Street, near the river, that Mildred shared with her
faculty friends Harold and Gladys Cook. It was a white clapboard eighteenth-century house with black shutters and a
little hedge out front; the front room where we met had a
nice old fireplace and worn Oriental carpets on the old floor-
boards, and shelves and shelves of books. Like young Nathan
Zuckerman, in *The Ghost Writer*, contemplating the living
room of the New England farmhouse of the writer E. I. Lon-
off, I would sit there on those darkening afternoons and—
while Pete, Dick, and I competed to outdo each other with
"insights"—say to myself, "This is how I will live." In just
such a house I would meet with my classes after I got my
Ph.D., became a teacher, and settled into a life of reading
books and writing about them. Tenure as an English professor
had come to seem a more realistic prospect than a career as
a novelist. I would be poor and I would be pure, a cross
between a literary priest and a member of the intellectual
resistance in Eisenhower's prospering pig heaven.

Here are a couple of Mildred Martin's notes from her diary for that year, and another of her memories.

Dec. 21, '53. When I was 21, in comparison with Roth and Minton, I was a child. I'm pleased with those two boys, and Tilton is working well, too. Susie Kriss hasn't been at the seminar for three weeks now, and Mrs. Bender has dropped. Mrs. Bender, after hearing Roth's paper on "The Fight at Finnsburgh," burst into tears and said she couldn't compete. She fled to the dining nook in the kitchen, where she could hear what was being said. At one point she came back, and said, "I know the answer to that question," answered correctly, and disappeared.

April 23, '54. Dismissed Sem. early, and the girls went fast, but the four boys just kept sitting, and we began to have a really good time. We stayed till 4:30, and then Roth came in to talk about his φβκ speech. A book sales-man came, the boys left, the salesman left, and Roth and Minton came back.

Memories. In the Lit. Library [the second-semester meeting place] there was an excited discussion about "the golden bird" near the end of "Sailing to Byzantium." Roth and Minton disagreed concerning its appropriate-ness. They rose, began shaking fists. Tasch, delighted, egged them on. I finally had to ask them to be seated. A unique experience.

The classroom had become my stage, usurping the maga-zine as a laboratory for self-invention and displacing the stu-dent drama group, Cap & Dagger, where I'd played supporting roles in ambitious student productions of *Oedipus Rex, School for Scandal,* and *Death of a Salesman.* Having brought to these parts more shamelessness than anything else, by my senior year I had even fewer illusions about becoming an actor than about turning into a Thomas Wolfe. Along with *Et Cetera*, Cap & Dagger had served me as an ersatz family, to take the place of the mainstream social fraternity from which I'd resigned. Though it was a respected organization, whose faculty advisers were among the most popular teachers on the campus, and though most of the student actors were just ordinary extroverted kids out to have a good time, it also harbored some mildly deviant types out to have a good time, as well as several campus misfits and artistic souls, whom I sometimes accompanied downtown for a beer or ate with at the men's dining hall.

It was there at Cap & Dagger that I found a steady girl-friend, Paula Bates, known as Polly, who came around to Bucknell Hall in the evenings to watch rehearsals or to prompt from the script or to act loosely as the director's assistant. She had arrived as a junior transfer student in my own junior year. She and her friend Margo Hand, who lived, as she did, in a room in French House, were the most sophisticated girls— and Polly was far and away the most sardonic girl—that I knew on campus. The well-brought-up daughter of a retired naval officer, she chain-smoked and drank martinis. The martinis impressed me when we first met and made me think of her as a woman of the world. She was frail and blond, not quite conventionally pretty, because of something slightly troubled in her expression, signifying, I think, the jagged overlap of the independent, no-nonsense wit who for months treated my declarations of feeling and my sexual persistence as an incomprehensible nuisance ("Stop *mooning*") with the delicate, kind, passionate girl whose parents' divorce and father's painful death had left her astonishingly susceptible to the intensity kindled by our affair.

The ordeal of overcoming Polly's wry skepticism was followed by the difficulties of finding a place to make love. We baby-sat for the Maurers and the Wheatcrofts and used their beds. We barricaded ourselves in a dormitory laundry room and lay on the cold floor. Vacations came, and back in New Jersey—where she stayed with her mother in Scotch Plains— I borrowed my father's car and we parked on dark, out-of-the-way streets. Over one Easter break someone lent us an apartment in New York for an afternoon and we luxuriated not only in the clandestine big-city hideaway and the feeling it gave us of being both free and on the run but also in finding ourselves unclothed together in a room full of sunlight. In the summer of 1953 we got jobs as counselors at a Jewish camp in the Poconos, where I had worked the year before, and there at night we took off for the woods. What with the obstacles to passion having to be surmounted again and again, our erotic life, along with the sheer thrill of its newness, had the underground piquancy of adultery. Even more than lovers, we became, through this drama of concealment and secrecy, the closest of companions and the most devoted of friends.

For my senior year I rented a room in town from an elderly widow, Mrs. Nellenback, white-haired and kindly-looking, a very strong Christian and, if I remember correctly, a Daughter of the American Revolution. Her simple white clapboard house, on a street corner not far from the women's quadrangle, was heavily laid with old carpets, and there were antimacassars and arm doilies on the upholstered furniture. The house was dark and quiet, with an unaired, not unpleasant smell of secure enclosure. The room I was offered was precisely what I wanted, potentially as much a love nest where Polly and I could stealthily retire to the narrow single bed as a scholar's secluded cell. I was duly informed on the day I rented the room that women were allowed in the house only on Sundays, when I could bring a fiancée for tea, provided the door to the hallway was left open. The room, which had once been the front parlor, was just off the main entryway on the first floor and had windows on two sides opening onto a summer porch that led down a little set of stairs to the quiet street. Since Mrs. Nellenback slept at the rear of the house—as did the housekeeper, a simpleminded woman who limped about with her feather duster, always smiling and singing babyish songs— and the other two roomers (one of them Pete Tasch) lived upstairs, it seemed to me that opportunities would abound for Polly to sneak in and out. After showing me the house, Mrs. Nellenback asked if I happened to be Armenian; I told her I was not. When I came back from studying at the library only a few nights after I'd moved in, I found on my bureau a plate with an apple and a cookie. When apples and cookies continued turning up, I knew I had a problem. How could I tell her to keep out of my room without making her suspicious of me as well as seeming ungrateful about the snack? And then again, now that we'd begun, how could I stop letting Polly in through the porch window after all the lights had gone out downstairs?

Several months after I'd moved in, Mrs. Nellenback took me aside one day as I was heading for my room and said, "I had a Jewish boy living here in 1939." I didn't know how to respond and said something like, "That's a long time ago." "Arthur Schwartz," she said, or some such name—"he was the nicest boy." Inside the room, with the door closed, I thought, *She knows*, meaning not that she knew that I was Jewish but that she, if not the readers of my *Et Cetera* fiction, knew that I wasn't entirely harmless.

We were caught a few weeks after the start of the second semester. I had thought, one Sunday evening, that Mrs. Nellenback had traveled the ten miles to Mifflinburg, as she often did, to visit her family, but apparently she had only gone for a visit in town, and she was home little more than an hour after she'd been driven away in her son's car. My shades were down, the room was black (and locked from the inside), and Polly and I were in bed. After the car had, surprisingly, pulled back up outside, and Mrs. Nellenback had come into the house and passed through the hallway just the other side of my door, we got up and, in the dark silence, groped about, dressing ourselves. Then the most sophisticated undergraduate couple at Bucknell tried their best to outsmart this elderly widow who never in her life had left Union County. I motioned for Polly to crawl under the bed and to hide there until I gave the all clear. Then I found a coat, grabbed a book, and, unlocking the door, stepped out of the dark room into the hallway. My plan was to be sure that no one was about, leave the house by the front door, and then from the porch quietly open the window so that Polly could step out and escape. Coming into the hallway, however, I found Mrs. Nellenback standing directly in front of me, still in her coat and hat. I was startled and she was grim. "Good evening," I said cheerily, and closed my door behind me. I couldn't lock it without giving everything away, and since she gave no sign of moving, I continued on out the front door and started walking toward the campus, book in hand, as though all along that had been my intention.

Some minutes later—already a little out of my mind from wandering aimlessly about—I saw Polly running up the street toward French House. She was in tears and could hardly speak. Mrs. Nellenback had waited only seconds for me to pass out of sight and then, having opened my unlocked door, turned on the light and made straight for the bed. "Get out of there, you hussy," she had said, poking with her foot under the bed, and Polly, covering her face with her hands, had rolled out from her hiding place and fled the room. Mrs. Nellenback followed her out onto the porch, threatening that she was going to have me thrown out of school.

The year was 1954 and the locale central Pennsylvania. She could do it. I took Polly to French House and then ran back to my room to find Mrs. Nellenback dialing the hall phone. I was sure that she was trying to reach the dean of men, who was no particular friend of mine since my assault on the *Bucknellian*. When I demanded that she speak to me, Mrs. Nellenback put down the phone and said, "I can have you thown out of the college for this." I replied loudly, "You had no right to scare that girl that way!" I was bluffing but didn't know what else to do except try to intimidate *her*. In the meantime I saw my life in a shambles. Polly's, too. Even though I intended to deny that it had been Polly who was in my room, I was sure the college authorities would haul her up for identification by Mrs. Nellenback. When this was over, I would have ruined not only my future but the future of the darling of the French department, who planned, like me, to begin graduate school in September.

It was the mid-1960s before I got round to exploiting this painful, ludicrous episode for a scene in my novel *When She Was Good*. The young couple there, Roy Bassart and Lucy Nelson, are extremely provincial small-town kids having virtually nothing in common with Polly and me. If anything, the drunkard's embittered Midwestern daughter Lucy has far more gritty rage with which to fight off her sense of shame than had the martini-drinking sophisticate from Scotch Plains, New Jersey. As for easygoing, unfocused, lackadaisical Roy, he hadn't any future at all to worry about losing. What happened to us, however, had a meaning very different; ours was a story about two intelligent, hopeful young people whose college success had given them everything to look forward to but whose infraction of the rules regulating their sexual lives rendered them, before the unlikely powers-that-be, just as powerless as a Roy and a Lucy.

I slept for a couple of nights at the Maurers', waiting to be summoned by the dean and subsequently sent home to Newark without a college degree (and for just the reason my father had always feared). When nothing happened, I took Bob Maurer's advice and quietly returned to my room and resumed my life at Mrs. Nellenback's. The incident was not mentioned by either of us, nor did I invite Polly to visit again, not even for tea, disguised as a fiancée. Afterward I couldn't figure out why Mrs. Nellenback had failed to make good on her threat—whether it was because she didn't want to be done out of the remaining rent and knew that with the second semester already under way it would be virtually impossible to replace me, or whether it had been an act of mercy by a good churchgoing woman, or whether I owed my luck to Arthur Schwartz, Bucknell '39.

For nearly six weeks early that spring we thought that Polly was pregnant. If she was, we didn't see how we could do anything but give up our graduate-school plans, marry, and stay on at Bucknell as salaried teaching assistants. We were in love, we were faculty favorites, Lewisburg living was cheap and simple, and it would even be possible to work toward an M.A. right there, though a second Bucknell degree was hardly what either of us had in mind. I had applied to go to Oxford or to Cambridge as a Fulbright or a Marshall scholar, and in the event that neither scholarship came through—unlikely, I thought, because I was near the top of my class—I had also put in for fellowships at three American universities; one was the University of Pennsylvania, where Polly planned to work on a Ph.D. Now we were as stunned to think that we might have to stay on at Bucknell indefinitely, living in the outlying university settlement, Bucknell Village, with the balding vets and their wives and babies—and our baby—as we'd been only a few months earlier, when we feared I was to be driven out of town for moral turpitude.

We would meet regularly for supper in the men's dining hall, where a number of nonsorority women also took their meals; Polly usually arrived first and waited for me by the door, and every evening when we caught sight of each other she'd shake her head, indicating that another day had passed without the onset of her period. Over our gravied Swiss steak and potatoes we'd buck each other up about the new and unexpected future as a married couple with a child and no money. I was reminded that as a father I wouldn't be drafted and have to waste two years of my life, after graduate school, as a private in the infantry. (Despite good relations with the colonel in charge of the Department of Military Science and Tactics, who had urged me to go on for a commission in the transportation corps of the post-Korea Army, I had quit ROTC, out of opposition to campus military training.) We tried to find some comfort in thoughts of the small, lively social circle of faculty people whom we liked to be with; certainly in the Maurers and the Wheatcrofts we had good and helpful friends, not really very much older than we were, with small children of their own. Heartbreaking as the situation was, and trapped as we felt, it seemed a test of maturity before which we simply could not bend; neither of us ever suggested that there was any other way out, at least not that early in the game.

Polly's discovery that she wasn't pregnant was my second pardon of the semester and filled us with enormous relief. For me it also turned out to be the beginning of the end of our affair. Having narrowly escaped premature domesticity and its encumbering responsibilities, I abandoned myself to dreams of erotic adventures that I couldn't hope to encounter other than on my own. I had successfully distanced myself at eighteen from my father's strictures, at nineteen from the meaningless affiliation to the Jewish fraternity, at twenty from the cozy ordinariness of the amiable student community; I had even begun to outgrow my own moralizing polemics. Now, at twenty-one, I wanted to be free from the exclusivity of monogamous love. The easiest way out would have been the offer of a scholarship to study literature in England, which we agreed I couldn't turn down; but though Fulbrights did go to two other Bucknell seniors, I was passed over for either scholarship that would have taken me abroad. The offer for a full fellowship did come, however, from the University of Pennsylvania, where Polly was to be a student too. There was also a fellowship from the graduate school of the University of Chicago. To Polly's astonishment—and somewhat even to my own—I hardened my heart and took the one from Chicago.

The summer after graduation we met one day to have lunch in New York and ended up arguing in Penn Station, where finally I told her the truth—and with about as much finesse as I'd displayed attacking the *Bucknellian*: I was passionately involved with another girl, whom I had met at a Newark day camp where I was working till I left for Chicago. I saw Polly again just once, two years later—with Jeffrey Lindquist, her husband-to-be, a good-looking, gentlemanly geology professor from Penn—while we were all coincidentally visiting the Maurers up in Maine. She married Jeffrey the next year, and eventually Paula Lindquist became a professor of French at New York University. She was forty-seven when she died of cancer, in 1979, only a few months after I had been back to Bucknell to receive an honorary degree. During my two days in Lewisburg—where I stayed with Emeritus Professor

Mildred Martin, who, for the processional march, accompanied me to the platform in her academic robes—I walked over to Mrs. Nellenback's to look at those porch windows leading to my old first-floor room. Needless to say, they were fewer and smaller than I'd remembered. It could never have been easy, in any way, getting in and out of them.

Girl of My Dreams

I'd noticed her long before that evening in Chicago when I introduced myself out on the street and persuaded her to have a cup of coffee with me in Steinway's drugstore, a university hangout only a few blocks from where she lived. Out of either shyness or savoir faire, I'd never in my life tried as blatantly to pick anybody up, which indicates not so much that fate had a hand in my trying now but that I was determined—as culturally inclined as I was psychologically resolved—to have my adventure with this woman who appeared to be the incarnation of a prototype.

In October 1956 I was not yet twenty-four, the Army was behind me, and my second published short story had been plucked from a tiny literary magazine and selected for Martha Foley's *Best American Short Stories* of 1956. I was an instructor (as well as a Ph. D. candidate) at the University of Chicago, I was sporting a tan glen-plaid Brooks Brothers University

Shop suit that I'd bought with Army separation pay in order to meet my college composition classes, and, having just come from a cocktail party at the Quadrangle Club for new faculty members, I had some four or five ounces of bourbon enkindling my flame. Roaring with confidence, then, and feeling absolutely free (". . . they were drunken, young, and twenty . . . and they knew that they could never die." T. Wolfe), I corralled her in the doorway of Woodworth's bookstore and said something like, "But you must have a cup of coffee with me—I know all about you." "Do you? What's there to know?" "You used to be a waitress in Gordon's." Gordon's was another university hangout, a restaurant just next door to Woodworth's. "Was I?" she replied. "You have two small children." "Do I?" "You come from Michigan." "And how do you know that?" "I asked. One day at Gordon's I saw your children with you. A little boy and a girl. About eight and six." "And just why have you bothered to remember all this?" "You seemed young to have those kids. I asked somebody and they told me you were divorced. They told me you were once an undergraduate here." "Not long enough for it to matter." "They told me your name. Josie. I came here as a graduate student in '54," I told her—"I used to have lunch at Gordon's. You waited on me and my friends." "I'm afraid I don't have that good a memory," she said. "I do," I replied, and doggedly witty, doggedly clever, doggedly believing myself utterly impregnable, I got her finally to accede—I would rarely ever get her to do that again—and to walk down the block and sit with me in a booth in the window of Steinway's. There the published young instructor presented his plumage in full, while Josie, quizzical and amused and flattered, said—in an ironic allusion to her powers to inflame—that she couldn't figure out what I was so fervent about.

But I was fervent then about almost everything, and that

evening fervent in the extreme because of those straight bour-
bons that I'd been drinking at the faculty-club party, where
I was the university's youngest new faculty member and ar-
guably its happiest. If she couldn't understand why the fervor
had fastened on her it was because what I experienced at
twenty-three as the power of a fascinating prototype felt to
her at twenty-seven like the sum of all her impediments. The
exoticism wasn't solely in her prototypical blue-eyed blond-
ness, though she was blue-eyed and very blond, a woman
whose squarish, symmetrical face, no matter how worn down
by furious combat, could still manage to look childlike and
tomboyish in a woolen ski hat; it wasn't in her prototypical
gentile appearance, though she was gentile-looking in a *volk-
isch* way that recalled nothing of the breezy bearing of brainy
Polly, with her sophisticated martinis and her sardonic refinement; it wasn't in her Americanness either, though her
speech and dress and manner made her a virtual ringer for
the solid, energetic girl in the cheery movies about America's
heartland, a friend of Andy Hardy's, a classmate of June Allyson's, off to the prom in his jalopy with Carleton Carpenter.
Though this hardly made her any less American, she was
actually a small-town drunkard's angry daughter, a young
woman already haunted by grim sexual memories and op-
pressed by an inextinguishable resentment over the injustice
of her origins; hampered at every turn by her earliest mistakes
and driven by fearsome need to bouts of desperate devious-
ness, she was a more likely fair-haired heroine for the scrutiny
of Ingmar Bergman than for the sunny fantasies of M-G-M.

What was exotic, then, wasn't the prototypical embodiment
of the Aryan gentile American woman—hundreds of young
women no less prototypical had failed to excite my interest
much at Bucknell—but, as I'd already sensed in Gordon's
restaurant back when she was still a newly divorced waitress

with two small kids and I was a U of C graduate student, that she was that world's *victim*, a dispossessed refugee from a sociobiological background to which my own was deemed, by both old- and new-world racial mythology, to be subservient, if not inferior. Had *her* father worked for the Metropolitan Life, he could have hoped to rise to be superintendent of agencies, or even dreamed of one day replacing the company president, whereas mine had deemed it necessary to risk our future in a business venture—and had the bad luck to come close to wrecking it—because the biggest financial institution in the world, the light of whose probity never failed, considered those of his religion best qualified for the lower levels of the corporate work force. Yet the fact was that her own father, a good-looking, former high school athlete named Smoky Jensen, had never been able to hold down a job successfully or give up the bottle and eventually wound up serving time for theft in a Florida jail, while my father, whose lack of education added to the handicap of his Jewish background, had by dint of his slavish energies and indestructible ambition reached a managerial rung on the Metropolitan Life hierarchy that, however insignificant in the company's overall organizational scheme, represented a real triumph of individual will over institutional bias. It was in large part Smoky Jensen's record as a father, a worker, a husband, and a citizen that had left Josie without the sustenance of family pride and bereft of affectionate attachment to the place where she'd been raised. She was adrift, not merely resentfully alienated from her Michigan upbringing but crudely and ambiguously amputated from her immediate ordeal as a wife and a mother; because of indebtedness and the fact that her semester and a half at Chicago qualified her for virtually no job that paid anything, she had worried ever since the end of her marriage about what would become of her on her own. Rooted most deeply in this pictorial embodiment of American Nordic root-edness was her hatred for her past and her fear of the future.

If our contrasting family endowments didn't accord with ancient racial mythology, they did conform to the simplifications about the inner resources of the Jews and the corrupting vices of the goyim that had sifted into my own sense of human subdivision from the beliefs of my Yiddish-speaking grandparents. Educated on their ancestors' and their own experience of violence, drunkenness, and moral barbarism among the Russian and Polish peasantry, these unworldly immigrants would not have imagined it to be quite as culturally illuminating as did their highly educated American grandson that a solid female specimen of earthy gentile stock could be blighted at the core by irresponsible parenting, involving not merely alcoholism and petty criminality but, as she would eventually allege, a half-realized attempt at childhood seduction. To them this would have seemed par for the course. Nor would they have found themselves anthropologically beguiled to learn that the divorced woman's own little boy and girl happened already to be enduring a childhood fate no less harsh than her own. It would simply have substantiated their belief in gentile family savagery to hear how her gentile husband (who, according to Josie's very dubious testimony, had "brow-beaten" her into conceiving the second child, just as he had "irresponsibly" knocked her up, a single girl starting college, to conceive the first) had "stolen" the two gentile children from their gentile mother and shipped them to be raised by others, more than a thousand miles from her arms, in Phoenix, Arizona. Despite her avowal of gruesome victimization at the hands of yet another merciless *shagitz*, my grandparents might even have surmised that the woman, having discovered that she was emotionally incapable of mothering anyone, had herself effectively let the two children go. She would have seemed to them nothing more or less than the legendary old-country shiksa-witch, whose bestial inheritance had doomed her to become a destroyer of every gentle human virtue esteemed by the defenseless Jew.

Raving within and stolidly blond without—Josie would have seemed to my grandparents the incarnation not of an American prototype but of their worst dream. And just *because* of that, their American grandson refused to be intimidated and, like a greenhorn haunted by the terrors of a vanished world, to react reflexively and run for his life. I was, to the contrary, thrilled by this opportunity to distinguish at first hand between American realities and shtetl legend, to surmount the instinctive repugnance of my clan and prove myself superior to folk superstitions that enlightened, democratic spirits like me no longer had dignified need of in the heterogeneous U.S.A. And to prove myself superior as well to Jewish trepidation by dint of taming the most fearsome female that a boy of my background might be unfortunate enough to meet on the erotic battlefield. What might signify a dangerous menace to the ghetto mentality, to me—with my M.A. in English and my new three-piece suit—looked as though it had the makings of a bracingly American amorous adventure. After all, the intellectually experimental, securely academic environs of Chicago's Hyde Park were as far as you could hope to get from the fears of Jewish Galicia.

During the day Josie worked as a secretary in the Division of Social Sciences, a job that she liked and that brought her into contact with distinguished visitors like Max Horkheimer, the Frankfurt sociologist, who enjoyed her company and sometimes took her to lunch or to the faculty club for a drink, and with a successful woman like Ruth Denney, the assistant to the dean of the division, who was only ten or so years older than Josie and whose professional achievement Josie vastly

admired though she realized a little bitterly that she was herself too far in the rear ever to hope to emulate it. The job
had helped enormously to get her readjusted to her new life
after the frantic period of near-breakdown following the loss
of her children. We met and became lovers just as she had
begun to enter the most hopeful period of her life since the
aborted undergraduate year at Chicago a decade earlier, when
she believed she had escaped Port Safehold, Michigan, and
everything there that threatened to destroy her.

Upon my return to Chicago, I'd lived first in a divinity-
school residence hall and then in a small apartment—one
room with a kitchen—a few blocks from the university. I went
off from there every weekday from 8:30 to 11:30 a.m. to teach
composition and, a couple of afternoons a week, to take
courses toward a Ph.D. in the graduate English department.
The other afternoons I sat squeezed in at my kitchen table,
where the daylight was stronger than it was anywhere else in
the minute flat, and wrote short stories on my portable Oli-
vetti. In the evenings I walked over to Josie's sizable railroad
flat in an old building near the IC tracks, carrying with me a
wad of freshman essays that I'd correct and grade in her living
room after we'd had dinner together and while she got on
with chipping away the layered paint to reach the bare pine
mantel of the fireplace. I thought it was game of her, after
her day at the office, to be laying new linoleum in the kitchen
and stripping the paper off the bathroom walls, and I admired
the enterprising way in which she partially met the costs of
the apartment—which had to be large, she said, so the children could visit during their Arizona school vacations—by
renting a back room to a happy-go-lucky premature hippie, a
U of C dropout, who, unfortunately, didn't always have money
for the rent. For me, the apartment and Josie's ambitions for
it placed her at the heart of the low-income Hyde Park style

of living that I found so congenial, blending as it did the neighborhood's unselfconscious strains of mildly disorderly bohemianism with the ordinary bourgeois taste for an attractive household where you could comfortably sit listening to music or reading a book or drinking cheap wine with your friends. In those years, nobody we knew wanted to own a television set, while every second person I met seemed to play the recorder.

Our evenings in Josie's apartment signaled to me that the aspiration that had carried me away from Newark and off to Bucknell at eighteen had been triumphantly realized at twenty-three (despite the fact that I was still a student and, except for my year in the Army, had been one since I was five): I was at last a man. It may be that why I dropped out of the Ph.D. program after little more than one quarter, why sitting in a class answering questions and going home to study for still more exams were all at once unendurable, had to do not just with deciding (largely because of my Martha Foley story) to stake my long-term future on writing fiction but with having gained the majority that I'd always known to be the goal of my education. At twenty-three I was independent of my family, though I still phoned them a couple of times a month, wrote occasional letters, and made the trek East at Christmastime to see them; I was settled into a desirable if tedious teaching position at a prestigious university in a city neighborhood where there were lots of secondhand bookstores and plenty of original intellectual types; and above all, I was conducting my first semidomesticated love affair where—even though their spectral presence was gigantic— nobody's parents were actually nearby, a love affair with a woman even more profoundly on her own than I was. That she was four years older than I seemed only further evidence of my maturity: our seemingly incompatible backgrounds attested to my freedom from the pressure of convention and my complete emancipation from the constraining boundaries protecting my preadult life. I was not only a man, I was a free man.

I thought then that I couldn't have found a more exhilarating intellectual arena than the University of Chicago in which to exercise my freedom to its utmost. After being discharged from the Army in August, I'd gone up to New York to begin looking for a job. Charlotte Maurer helped get me an interview at the *New Yorker*, and through the influence of the novelist Charles Jackson, who wrote copy at the J. Walter Thompson advertising agency, where my brother was then an art director, I had gotten to see Roger Straus, Jackson's publisher, who twenty years later became my own publisher. A few days after the interviews, I was elated to find myself being offered two jobs—as a copy editor at Farrar, Straus, and Cudahy and as a checker at the *New Yorker*. Before I could choose between them, however, a telegram arrived unexpectedly from Napier Wilt, a former teacher of mine and dean of humanities at Chicago; at the last minute a position had opened up on the freshman composition staff of the college, and Wilt was asking if I was interested in joining the Chicago faculty as an instructor in September.

Not only did I consider university teaching worthwhile, interesting work, but it was clear that of the three jobs the instructorship would afford the most opportunity to write: even with three composition sections, each meeting five hours a week, I'd still have as much as half of each day left for myself, and then there'd be quarterly breaks, periodic holidays, and summer vacations. All that free time was particularly appealing after my claustrophobic months in the Army. Following basic training at Fort Dix, I'd been assigned to Washington to serve as a private writing news handouts for the public-

information officer of Walter Reed Army Hospital. (Because
of a back injury sustained at Dix, I eventually wound up a
patient in the hospital and, after two months in bed there,
was released from the service with a medical discharge.)
Working in the public-information office for more than half a
year provided my first taste of the tedium of a nine-to-five
job; the work was hardly demanding, but there were still days
when being cooped up for eight hours, mindlessly banging a
typewriter, nearly drove me nuts. Consequently, once I was
free of the Army enclosure, I seized on this chance to rise
from former graduate student to university instructor and to
return to Chicago, once again to argue about books and theo-
rize to my heart's content about literature and, what's more,
to live on practically nothing (that's about what the job paid)
without feeling like a pauper, which you could do in those
days around a university. In 1956, at twenty-three, I saw the
University of Chicago as the best place in America to enjoy
maximum personal freedom, to find intellectual liveliness, and
to stand, if not necessarily in rebellious opposition, at least at
a heartening distance from the prospering society's engross-
ment with consuming goods and watching TV.

EVER SINCE THE SUMMER of my Bucknell graduation I'd been
carrying in my wallet the photograph of a college student from
suburban north Jersey, a Jewish girl whose family history and
personal prospects couldn't have been less like Josie's; she
was quick-witted, intelligent, and vivacious, quite pretty, and
possessed of the confidence that's often the patrimony of a
young woman adored since birth by a virile, trustworthy,
successful father. Harry Milman, Gayle's father, made not the
slightest attempt to disguise the impassioned pride he took
in his four children, toward whom he was unfailingly affec-

tionate and generous; he was a hard-driving, rough-hewn busi-
nessman, like my own father out of Jewish immigrant Newark,
and in those years when Gayle was still his loving dependent
daughter, he loomed in the background of her life as an im-
pressively protective figure. The bond to her mother, a very
good-looking woman in her early fifties, had by then begun
to chafe an adventurous girl of eighteen and nineteen, yet the
relationship, if at times strained, was never in real danger of
deteriorating into anything unmanageably painful. The hall-
marks of the family were solidarity and confidence. Could
Josie have been disarmed of her resentful defiance and permitted to press her nose up against the glass of the picture
window of the Milmans' large suburban house, she might well
have stood there weeping with envy and wishing with all her
heart to have been transformed into Gayle. She magically
sought something approximating that implausible metamor-
phosis by deciding to marry me against all reasonable resistance and, on top of that, to become a Jew.

"Oh," cries Peter Tarnopol in *My Life as a Man*, pining for
the Sarah Lawrence senior whom he'd cast off in favor of his
angry nemesis, "why did I forsake Dina Dornbusch—for Maureen!" Why did *I* forsake Gayle for Josephine Jensen? Over
a period of some two years, while I was in graduate school
and in the Army, Gayle and I were equally caught up by an
obsessional passion yet, returning to Chicago in September
1956, I thought my voyage out—wherever it might be taking
me—could no longer be impeded by this affair, which, as I
saw it, had inevitably to resolve into a marriage linking me
with the safe enclosure of Jewish New Jersey. I wanted a
harder test, to work at life under more difficult conditions.

The joke on me was that Gayle had an enigmatic adventure
of her own to undertake and, after graduating from college,
propelled by the very gusto and self-assurance that had ger-

minated in the haven of her father's hothouse, for over a decade led a single life in Europe whose delights had little in common with the pleasures of her conventional upbringing. From the stories that reached me through mutual friends, it sounded as though Harry Milman's daughter had become the most desirable woman of *any* nationality between the Berlin Wall and the English Channel; meanwhile, the outward-bound voyager who refused to curb his precious independence by even the shadow of a connection with the provincial world he'd outgrown had sealed himself into a joyless existence, rife with the most preposterous, humanly meaningless responsibilities.

I had got everything backward. Josie, with her chaotic history, seemed to me a woman of courage and strength for having survived that awful background. Gayle, on the other hand, because of all that family security and all that father love, seemed to me a girl whose comfortable upbringing would keep her a girl forever. Gayle would be dependent because of her nurturing background and Josie would be independent because of her broken background! Could I have been any more naïve? Not neurotic, naïve, because that's true about us too: very naïve, even the brightest, and not just as youngsters either.

THREE CLOSE FRIENDSHIPS that I made at the university during my first months back in Chicago were with the novelists Richard Stern and Thomas Rogers and the critic and editor Ted Solotaroff. The three of them were four to five years older than I and already married—Dick and Ted each had a couple of small children—but we were all still only in our twenties and wanted to be writers. Dick and Tom were new members of the U of C faculty, while Ted was teaching evening classes down at an Indiana University extension in Gary and studying as I was in the Chicago Ph.D. program. Josie and I would see the Sterns or the Rogerses or the Solotaroffs fairly regularly for dinner or a poker game or a beer, and the camaraderie made us seem something like a married couple ourselves, even if I was more aware than ever, particularly from the example of Ted's difficult life and the obvious strain that a family imposed on his time to write and to pursue his degree, that for financial reasons alone my own writing ambition would best be served by being responsible for only myself. Though my salary was $2,800 a year, I was still trying to save toward the European journey that seemed to me very much a part of a literary apprenticeship. I was almost certain that I could never expect to live on my earnings as a writer, even if eventually I came to be published in large-circulation magazines as well as in the literary quarterlies that were my natural home in those days. It went without saying (certainly at the University of Chicago) that one did not write in the *expectation* of making money. I thought that if I was ever pressed to write for money, I wouldn't be able to write at all.

During the first months Josie and I were together I talked much of the time about writing, bought her my favorite paperbacks, loaned her heavily underlined Modern Library copies of the classics, read aloud pages from the novelists I admired, and began after a while to show her the manuscripts of the stories I was working on. When I was asked to contribute movie reviews to the *New Republic* at $25 a shot (a job offered to me as a result of a little satire about Eisenhower's evening prayer that the *New Republic* had reprinted from the *Chicago Review*), we went to the films together and talked about them on the way home. Over dinner we educated each other about those dissimilar American places from which we'd emerged, she badly impeded and vulnerable—and only now sufficiently

free to try valiantly to recover her equilibrium and make a
new life as an independent woman—and I, from the look of
it, fortified, intact, and hungry for literary distinction. The
stories I told of my protected childhood might have been
Othello's tales about the men with heads beneath their shoul-
ders, so tantalized was she by the atmosphere of secure, de-
pendable comfort that I ascribed to my mother's genius for
managing our household affairs and to the dutiful persever-
ance of both my parents even in their years of financial strain.
I spoke of the artistry practiced within my mother's kitchen
with no less enthusiasm than when I enlightened her about
the sensuous accuracy of *Madame Bovary*. Because the grade
and high schools I attended had been virtually down the street
from our house, I had as a boy gone home for lunch every
day—the result, I told her, was that after I'd returned from
teaching my morning classes and changed from my new suit
into my old writing clothes the first whiff of Campbell's tomato
soup heating up in the kitchen of my little Chicago flat could
still arouse the coziest sense of anticipation and imminent,
satisfying consummation, yielding what I had only recently
learned to recognize as a "Proustian" thrill (despite my in-
ability during consecutive summers to get beyond page 60 of
Swann's Way).

Was I exaggerating? Did I idealize? I don't know—did
Othello? Winning a new woman with one's narratives, one
tends not to worry about what I once heard an Englishman
describe as "overegging the custard." I think now that what
encouraged me to disclose in such loving detail a memory I
wouldn't have dreamed of exploiting while wooing a confident,
well-brought-up girl like Polly Bates, whose faith in her origins
was unchallengeable—and that would have been entirely beside the point with Gayle Milman, the daughter of a Jewish
household far more of a lotus land to its offspring than my

own—was an innate taste for dramatic juxtaposition, an infatuation with the coupling of seemingly alien perspectives. My unbroken progress from the hands of the *mohel* to Mildred Martin, my history as the gorged beneficiary of overdevotion, overprotection, and oversurveillance within an irreproachably respectable Jewish household, was recounted in alternating sequence with her own life stories and formulated, I think, as a moral antidote to flush from her system the poisonous residue still tainting her belief in the possibilities for fulfillment. I was wooing her, I was wowing her, I was spiritedly charming her—motivated by an egoistic young lover's predilection for intimacy and sincerity, I was telling her who I thought I was and what I believed had formed me, but I was also engaged by a compelling form of narrative responsory. I was a countervoice, an antitheme, providing a naïve challenge to the lurid view of human nature that emerged from her tales of victimized innocence, first as an only child raised from her earliest years as the not entirely welcome guest—along with her long-suffering mother and semiemployable father—in the house of her Grandfather and Stepgrandmother Hebert and then at the hands of the high school sweetheart whom she'd married and whom she had reason, she told me, to despise forever.

She would despise him forever. I was as hypnotized—and flooded with chivalric fantasies of manly heroism—by her unforgiving hatred of all the radically imperfect gentile men who she claimed had abused her and had come close to ruining her as she was enchanted—and filled with fantasy—by my Jewish idyll of neatly ironed pajamas and hot tomato soup and what that promised about the domestication, if not the sheer feminizing, of unmuzzled maleness. The more examples she offered of their irresponsible, unprincipled conduct, the more I pitied her the injustices she had had to endure and admired the courage it had taken to survive. When she reviled them with that peculiarly potent adjective of hers, "wicked"—which I till then had associated primarily with people like the defendants at Nuremberg—the nearer I felt drawn to a world from which I no longer wished to be sheltered and about which a man in my intended line of work ought really to know something: the menacing realms of benighted American life that so far I had only read of in the novels of Sherwood Anderson and Theodore Dreiser. The more graphically she illustrated their callow destructiveness of every value that my own family held dear, the more contempt I had for them and the more touching examples I provided of our exemplary history of harmlessness. I could as well have been working for the Anti-Defamation League—only instead of defending my minority from anti-Semitic assaults on their good name and their democratic rights, I cast myself as the parfit Jewish knight dispatched to save one of their own from the worst of the gentile dragons.

Four months after we'd met Josie discovered she was pregnant. I couldn't understand how it had happened, since even when she claimed it was a safe time of the month and saw no need for contraception, I insisted on her using a diaphragm. We were both stunned, but the doctor, an idealistic young neighborhood GP who had been treating Josie at very modest rates, came around to her apartment to confirm it. Sitting gloomily over coffee with him in the kitchen, I asked if there was any way to abort the pregnancy. He said that all he could do was try a drug that at this stage sometimes induced heavy bleeding that then required hospitalization for a D&C. The chances were slim that it would work—but astoundingly it did; in a matter of days Josie began to hemorrhage, and I took her to the hospital for the scraping. When she was back in her room later in the day I returned to visit, bearing a bunch of flowers and a bottle of domestic champagne. I found her in bed, as contented-looking as a woman who had given birth to a perfect child and talking brightly to a middle-aged man who turned out to be not a member of the medical staff but a rabbi who served as one of the hospital chaplains. After he and I exchanged pleasantries, the rabbi left her bedside so that Josie and I could be alone. I said to her suspiciously, "What was he doing here?" Perfectly innocently she replied, "He came to see me." "Why you?" "On the admissions form," she said, "under religion, I wrote 'Jewish.'" "But you're not Jewish." She shrugged, and in the circumstances I didn't know what more to say. I was perplexed by what seemed to me her screwy mix of dreaminess and calculation, yet still so relieved that we were out of trouble that I dropped the interrogation, got some glasses, and we drank to our great good luck.

Two years later she turned up pregnant again. By then we no longer had anything resembling a love affair, only a running feud focused on my character flaws and from which I was finding it impossible to escape no matter how far I fled. I had spent the summer of 1958 traveling by myself in Europe and, instead of returning to Chicago, had quit my job and moved to Manhattan. I had found an inexpensive basement apartment on the Lower East Side and was living off the first payment of the $7,500 fellowship Houghton Mifflin had just awarded me for the manuscript of *Goodbye, Columbus*, which they were to publish in the spring of 1959. I had left Chicago for good in May after a year in which the deterioration of trust between Josie and me had elicited the most grueling, draining, bewildering quarrels: her adjective "wicked" did not sound so alluring when it began to be used to describe me. Except for unavoidable encounters around the university neighborhood, half of the time we didn't see each other at all, and for a while, after we had seemingly separated for good,

I became enamored of a stylish Radcliffe graduate, Susan Glassman, who was living with her prosperous family on the North Shore and taking graduate classes in English at Chicago. She was a beautiful young woman who seemed to me all the more desirable for being a little elusive, though actually I didn't like too much that I couldn't entirely seem to claim her attention. One afternoon I dealt the final blow to whatever chances I had with Susan by asking her to come along with me to hear Saul Bellow speak at the Hillel House. Josie happened to have taken the afternoon off from work and to my dismay was in the audience too; but as Bellow was one of my literary enthusiasms that she'd come to share, neither of us should really have been as surprised as we appeared to be by the other's presence. After the talk, Susan went off to introduce herself to Bellow; they had met once through mutual friends at Bard, and, as it turned out, in those few minutes a connection was reestablished that would lead in a couple of years to her becoming Bellow's third wife. Josie, who'd come to the Hillel House on her own, superciliously looked my way while Susan was standing and talking to Bellow; when I came over to say hello, she muttered, with a sharp little laugh, "Well, if *that's* what you like—!" There was nothing to say to that, and so I just walked off again and waited to take Susan out for a drink with the Solotaroffs. Later in the evening, when I got back to my apartment, I found a scribbled note in my mailbox, tellingly succinct—and not even signed—to the effect that a rich and spoiled Jewish clotheshorse was exactly what I deserved.

What I discovered when I returned from Europe in September 1958 was that, having spent July and August working in New York for *Esquire*, Josie had decided against returning to Chicago and her secretarial job at the university. She'd enjoyed Manhattan and her position at the fringe of the literary life and had decided to stay on "in publishing," for which she had no qualifications aside from the little experience at *Esquire*. But if I was Jewish she was Jewish, if I lived in Manhattan she lived in Manhattan, if I was a writer she was a writer, or would at least "work" with writers. It turned out that during the summer she had let on to some of the magazine people she'd met that she had "edited" my stories that had begun to appear in *Commentary* and the *Paris Review*. When I corrected her and said that though she certainly read them and told me what she thought, that was not what was meant by "editing," she was affronted: "But it is—I am your editor!"

The quarreling started immediately. Because of her desperation at finding herself purposeless in New York and unwanted by me, the exchanges were charged with language so venomous that afterward I would sometimes wind up out on the street wandering around alone for hours as though it were *my* life that had hit bottom. She located an apartment to sublet, moved in, and then mysteriously the apartment was lost; she found a job, turned up for work—or said she did—and then mysteriously there was no job. Her little reserve of money was running out, she had nowhere permanent to live, and none of her job interviews seemed ever to yield anything real. Repeatedly she would get on the wrong subway and call from phone booths in Queens or Brooklyn, panting and incoherent, begging me to come get her.

I didn't know what to do or whom to turn to. I was new to New York myself, and the only person I could have confided in was my brother. After all, it was in the paperback books that he brought home on weekends from Pratt Institute when he was an art student there that I had got my first glimpse of serious modern fiction. What's more, when I was fourteen and fifteen, and he was filling his student sketchbooks with slices of urban landscape and rapid portraits of seedy city dwellers, his determination to seek an artistic vocation wasn't without its inspiring effect. His diligent example established in my own mind the understanding that an insurance man's son had the right—if he had the talent and industry—to pursue something other than a conventional career in business or the professions. Why my father never seriously questioned Sandy's decision or tried in any serious way to alter his course—or to interfere later with my aspirations—may have something to do with the example of my mother's brother, Mickey, if one can even speak of the influence of a mild, mordantly humorous loner who would never have presumed to advocate his way of life to anyone, least of all to my brother, to whom he passed on some of his cherished old anatomy books but whom he dryly warned of the impossibility of being a good artist, let alone making a living as one. Nonetheless, the precedent that our Uncle Mickey furnished made painting seem to the family not so much a curiosity as a real line of work; whether it was a desirable line of work was something else—Mickey's shabby, comfortless existence in his small Philadelphia studio would intermittently arouse my father's ire, and he would harangue our poor mother at dinner about how her brother ought at least to go out and find himself a girl to marry. The freedom that Sandy and I felt in experimenting with work so far outside the local cultural orbit probably had also to do with the fact that our father, lacking a real education himself, was, luckily for us, deficient in specific ideas about what vocations his sons might best aspire to. He wanted mainly for us not to be wanting, and that we could accomplish by hard work.

Though Sandy and I sometimes *felt* as though we had a lot to say to each other, in the years after I came out of the Army, we began to be drawn apart by the sentiments and interests predictably associated with our work, his as a commercial artist at an advertising agency and mine as a college instructor and novice writer. When we were together I did my best to suppress my disdain (not inconsiderable in my twenties and the Eisenhower fifties) for the advertising man's point of view; but he was hardly less aware of it than I was of his uneasiness around university types and highbrow intellectuals or of the provocation that he sensed in what he took to be their pretensions. This was not, of course, a major concern of his, and it unsettled his general equilibrium as little as the agenda of J. Walter Thompson Co. seriously interfered with how I lived; still, a suspicious undercurrent between us, fostered by strong professional polarities, made for self-consciousness and even shyness when we met or telephoned. On top of that, Josie and Sandy's wife, Trudy, couldn't stand each other, and so we had no more reason to go out and socialize as couples than to sit down together and talk intimately—"like brothers," as my father would have advised. Because Sandy was embarked on a marriage and a career pointing him in a more conventional direction than mine, planning the sort of life that looked to me to have more obviously evolved from the background I'd put behind me, it didn't seem to me that he would have had the wherewithal—"morally," as I would have been quick to say then—to help me through my predicament or, if he did, that it was possible for *me* with *my values*, to solicit his assistance. This was hubris, pure and simple, the arrogance of a young literary mentality absolutely assured of its superior wisdom, as well as the pride of a raw recruit of a man, vigorously intent on being independent, who could not confess to an older, seemingly less adventurous brother that he was being dragged beyond his depth and needed someone strong to save him.

Besides, I was the strong one, was I not? I still believed that, and not entirely without reason: these were the most triumphant months of my life. Less than five years out of college, I was about to have a first book published, and my editors at Houghton Mifflin, George Starbuck and Paul Brooks, were tremendously encouraging; on the basis of a few published stories, I had already established a small reputation in New York, and through new friendships with Martin Greenberg at *Commentary*, Robert Silvers at *Harper's*, George Plimpton at the *Paris Review*, Rust Hills at *Esquire*, and Aaron Asher at Meridian Books, I was meeting other writers and beginning to enjoy feeling like a writer myself instead of like a freshman-composition teacher who'd written a few short stories on the side. This spent love affair with Josie, a shambles for nearly a year now, couldn't possibly bring down someone on my trajectory. It wasn't marriage I was worried about, marriage was inconceivable: I just didn't want her to have a breakdown and, though I couldn't believe she would do it, I dreaded the possibility that she might kill herself. She had begun to talk about throwing herself in front of a subway car— and what seemed to have exacerbated her hopelessness was my new literary recognition. "It isn't fair!" she cried. "You have everything and I have nothing, and now you think you can dump me!"

Whether appropriately or not, I felt responsible for her having come to New York that summer. The temporary *Esquire* opening was as a reader for Gene Lichtenstein and Rust Hills, the magazine's fiction editors; when Josie had heard of the job and expressed interest in it, I had assured Gene and Rust she could do it—I figured that if she got it, it might help, if only temporarily, to quiet her complaint about going nowhere in life. I suppose I thought of this as the last thing I would try to help her out with before I disappeared completely. Later she was to claim that if Rust Hills hadn't promised her that the job would become permanent after the

summer she would never have left Chicago; she would also
have returned to Chicago if I hadn't implied, in letters that
I'd written her from Europe, that I wanted her to stay on
after I got back to New York. Rust Hills and I had both misled
her, and when she turned up at the dock to meet my boat at
the end of August 1958, it was because *she* knew that's what
I'd wanted. Waving excitedly from the pier in a white summer
dress, she looked very like a bride. Maybe that was the idea.

We spent a couple of endurable evenings during the following weeks with a young English architect whom I'd met
on the boat and his English girlfriend, who was working in
New York for *Vogue* at just the kind of job Josie wanted but
couldn't seem to get. One of those nights we attempted to
make love in my basement apartment; that I was pretty obviously without desire put her into a rage about "all the girls
you screwed in Europe." I didn't deny that I hadn't been
chaste while I was traveling—"Why should I have been?" I
asked—thus making things predictably worse. By November
she was wandering around New York with no money and
nowhere of her own to live, and eventually, when she wound
up one cold morning standing with her suitcase at the foot of
the cracked concrete stairs leading down to my apartment and
demanding that I summon up just one iota of compassion and
give her a place to stay, it occurred to me to abandon the
apartment to her—forget my records and my books and the
few hundred dollars' worth of secondhand furniture, and disappear with what remained of my Houghton Mifflin money.
But there was a two-year lease on the $80-a-month apartment
to which I'd signed my name, there were my parents in New
Jersey, whom I spoke to on the phone weekly and who were
delighted that I appeared to be permanently settled back
East—and there was the promise of my new life in Manhattan.
There was also my refusal to run away. Fleeing and hiding

were repugnant to me: I still believed that there were certain character traits distinguishing me from the *truly* wicked bastards out of her past. "You and Rust Hills and my father!" she shouted, weeping outside the doorway at the bottom of that dark well—"You're all exactly the same!" It was the craziest assertion I had ever heard, and yet, as though I had no choice but to take the accusation seriously and prove myself otherwise, instead of running I stayed. So did she. With me.

So the second time she turned up pregnant was early in February 1959. I won't describe our life together on the Lower East Side during the three preceding months except to say that I'm as surprised today as I was then that we didn't wind up—one or both of us—maimed or dead. She produced the perfect atmosphere in which I couldn't think. By the beginning of the year in which *Goodbye, Columbus* was to be published, I was nearly as ripe for hospitalization as she was, my basement apartment having all but become a psychiatric ward with café curtains.

How she could be pregnant was even harder to understand this time than it had been in Chicago the year before, when it never occurred to me that the pregnancy had resulted from her failing to use the diaphragm she invariably purported to be going off to the bathroom to insert. She already had two children she couldn't raise and grievously missed—why would she go out of her way to have a third? Four months after we'd met there'd been no reason to question her honesty—unless, of course, instead of swallowing whole her story of relentless victimization, instead of being so beguiled by the proximity she afforded me to the unknown disorders of gentile family life—to those messy, sordid, unhappy realities that inspired my grandparents' goy-hating legends—I'd had the know-how at twenty-four to cast as cold an eye on her self-presentation as she did on the men who had been abusing her all her life.

It was true that in the middle of the night there had been two, three, even perhaps four fantasy-ridden, entangled couplings in which we had somehow slaked our anger and, somnambulistically, eased the physical hunger aroused by the warm bed and the pitch-black room and the discovery of an identityless human form among the disheveled bedclothes. In the full light of morning I would wonder if what I seemed to remember had not been enacted in a dream; on the February morning that she announced she was pregnant once again, I could have sworn that for weeks and weeks I hadn't even *dreamed* such an encounter—I was erotically too mummified even for that. I had just come back from Boston, where I had been seeing to the galleys of my book with George Starbuck, and it was more or less with the news of her pregnancy that she greeted my return: not only was I on the brink of being the author of a first collection of stories, I was scheduled to become a father as well. It was a lie, I knew the moment she said it that it was a lie, and I believed that what had prompted the lie was her desperation over my Boston trip, her fear that with the publication of my first book, which was only months away, my conscience would be catapulted beyond the reach of her accusations, my self-esteem elevated to heights that would have situated her too—if only she was at my side—high above the hell of all that failure.

When I told her that it was impossible for her to be pregnant again, she repeated that she was indeed going to have a baby and that, if I "wickedly" refused to be responsible for it, she would carry it to term and leave it on my parents' doorstep in New Jersey.

I didn't think she was incapable of doing that (had she been pregnant, that is), for by this time she was nursing a grievance against my parents too—she claimed they'd treated her "ruthlessly" during a disastrous visit she'd made to our house two summers earlier. I had gone off to spend a month by myself writing in a rented room on Cape Cod; at the end of the month, as prearranged, Josie had come out from Chicago for a week's vacation. On the Falmouth beach one afternoon a week after my arrival, I'd met a Boston University senior, a quiet, easygoing, plainish girl, an elementary-education student who was waiting on tables at a seafood house; soon we were sleeping together and spending her afternoons off walking the beach and swimming. Her boyfriend wanted to marry her when she graduated but she wasn't sure marriage was a good idea; I told her that I had a friend coming to visit whom I didn't want to see either. Our troublesome, ambiguous affairs were what we mostly had in common, that and desire for a brief respite from their problems. We were able to say goodbye relatively easily, but when I drove to Boston to pick Josie up at the airport and take her back down to the Cape, the aftershock of the agreeable few weeks with the B.U. girl, the sense of loss I felt for someone I barely knew but with whom things had been so pleasant, was stronger than I could have anticipated, and with Josie I immediately registered my disappointment at the prospect of resuming all the debilitating old quarrels—which, of course, guaranteed their immediate resumption.

Within seventy-two hours things were as hellish as they'd ever been, and we called it quits and drove to New York. She was going to finish out the week in a hotel there, seeing the sights on her own, while I went on to New Jersey—to Moorestown, near Camden, where my father had lately been transferred to manage the Metropolitan's local district office. I planned to stay in Moorestown for a week before returning to my job in Chicago. Josie knew that Polly had spent Thanksgiving with my family one November and that she had stayed for a part of the Easter break when we were seniors at Bucknell; on the drive down from the Cape, she insisted on knowing why she couldn't come along—what had made Polly Bates so special? How could I treat her so wretchedly after she'd spent her savings coming all the way to Cape Cod to see me? Wasn't I grown up enough to introduce to my mother and father the woman with whom I'd lived for a year in Chicago? Was I a man or was I a child? When she wouldn't stop I wanted to kill her. Instead I took her home with me.

That she wasn't Jewish hardly entered into it—neither had Polly been Jewish, but my parents were always cordial to her, had fully expected me to marry her, and, after we went our separate ways to graduate school, asked me often if I knew how she was doing and remembered her affectionately. No, what they saw to frighten them wasn't the shiksa but a hard-up loser four years my senior, a penniless secretary and divorced mother of two small children, who, as she was quick to explain at dinner the first night, had been "stolen" from her by her ex-husband. While my mother was in the laundry room doing the family wash the next morning, Josie came in with her dirty clothes from her few days on the Cape and asked if my mother minded if she threw them into the machine too. The last thing that my mother wanted anything to do with was this woman's soiled underwear, but as hopelessly polite as the ideal housewife in her favorite women's magazines, she said, "Of course, dear," and obligingly put them into the wash. Then she walked all the way to my father's office, some three miles away, weeping in despair over what I, with all my prospects, was doing with this obviously foundering woman who bore no resemblance to Polly or Gayle, and certainly none to her. She had seen instantly what was wrong, everything that it had taken months for me even to begin to recognize, every disaster-laden thing from which I was unable to sever myself—and toward which I continued to feel an overpowering, half-insane responsibility. My mother could not be consoled; once again Josie was furious and affronted; and my father, with extreme diplomacy, with a display of gentlemanly finesse that revealed to me, maybe for the first time in my life, the managerial skills for which he was paid by the Metropolitan Life, tried to explain to her that his wife had meant her no harm, that they had been pleased to meet her, but that it might be best for everyone if Philip took her to the airport the next day.

I was desolated, particularly since what happened was just what I'd expected—this was precisely why I hadn't wanted her to come with me. And yet on the drive down, when she'd told me how miserable she would be alone in a cheap New York hotel or, worse still, back in hot Chicago, having had, because of me, the worst possible vacation, I had once again been unable to say no—just as I'd been unable to tell her that I hadn't wanted her to join me for as little as a day when I'd first decided to go off that summer for a month on Cape Cod. I could have spared Josie her humiliation, I could have spared my mother her unhappiness—and myself my mounting confusion—if only I hadn't been so frightened of appearing heartless in the face of her unrelenting need and everything that was owed to her.

It was no wonder—though maybe it was nothing less than that, given my enslavement to her sense of victimization—that, when I did get back to Chicago that fall, we were together less and less, and I began to resume a vigorous bachelor life, pursuing Susan Glassman and intermittently dating a perfectly sane editorial assistant for the *Bulletin of the Atomic Scientists*, whom, had I settled in for good in Chicago, I would probably have seen much more of. Bizarrely, had I remained in Chicago, where Josie was installed in her job and her apartment, instead of rushing to put a thousand miles between myself and our hopeless estrangement, she would never have wound up alone in Manhattan, positioned to throw herself on me as all that stood between her and ruination. But not foreseeing that was the least of what I didn't know, brainy young fellow that I was on my Houghton Mifflin literary fellowship.

The description in *My Life as a Man*, in the chapter "Marriage à la Mode," of how Peter Tarnopol is tricked by Maureen Johnson into believing her pregnant parallels almost exactly how I was deceived by Josie in February 1959. Probably nothing else in my work more precisely duplicates the autobiographical facts. Those scenes represent one of the few occasions when I haven't spontaneously set out to improve on actuality in the interest of being more interesting. I couldn't have been more interesting—I couldn't have been *as* interesting. What Josie came up with, altogether on her own, was a little gem of treacherous invention, economical, lurid, obvious, degrading, deluded, almost comically simple, and best of all, magically effective. To reshape even its smallest facet would have been an aesthetic blunder, a defacement of her life's single great imaginative feat, that wholly original act which freed her from the fantasied role as my "editor" to become, if for a moment only, a literary rival of audacious flair, one of those daringly "pitiless" writers of the kind Flaubert found most awesome, the sort of writer my own limited experience and orderly development prevented me then from even beginning to resemble—masterly pitilessness was certainly nowhere to be found in the book of stories whose publication she so envied and to which she was determined to be allied. In a fifteen-page explication of human depravity by one of his garrulous, ruined, half-mad monologists, Dostoevsky himself might not have been ashamed to pay a hundred-word tribute to the ingenuity of that trick. For me, however, it was to become something more fateful than a sordid little footnote

to somebody else's grandiose epic of evil, since by the time
she came to confess to me two and a half years later (and,
rather as Maureen makes her disclosure to Tarnopol, drugged
and drunk, midway through a botched suicide attempt), by
the time I learned from her how she had played her trick in
Manhattan—as well as how she'd used no contraception in
Chicago—we had repeatedly been in court to try to wrest her
children back from her first husband. By then her daughter,
a harassed, endearing, well-intentioned, ill-educated, emotionally abused girl of ten, was living in our house in Iowa
City, and Josie was threatening to stab me to death in my
sleep if I should ever attempt to seduce the child, whom in
fact I was hoping, literally, to teach to tell time and to read.
Needless to say, to *this* development Dostoevsky might have
allowed something more than a mere one hundred words. I
myself allowed several thousand words to find an apposite,
deserving setting for her scenario in the opening section of
My Life as a Man, in the chapter "Courting Disaster," which
purports to be Peter Tarnopol's macabre fictional transmog-
rification of his own awful-enough "true story." For me, if not
for the reader, that chapter—indeed the novel itself—was
meant to demonstrate that my imaginative faculties had managed to outlive the waste of all that youthful strength, that
I'd not only survived the consequences of my devastating case
of moral simpletonism but finally prevailed over my grotesque
deference to what this wretched small-town gentile paranoid
defined as my humane, my manly—yes, even my Jewish—
duty.

The urine specimen that she submitted to the drugstore
for the rabbit test was purchased for a couple of dollars from
a pregnant black woman she'd inveigled one morning into a
tenement hallway across from Tompkins Square Park. Only
an hour earlier she'd left my apartment, ostensibly for the

drugstore, with a bottle in her purse containing her own urine, but as that would have revealed her to be *not* pregnant, it was useless for her purpose. Tompkins Square Park looked run-down even in those days but was still back then a perfectly safe place, a neighborhood resting spot for the elderly, where they sat in good weather and talked and read their newspapers—more often than not, papers in Ukrainian—and where the local young mothers, many of them very young and Puerto Rican, brought their children to play and run about. After a day of writing, I'd either walk over with my own newspaper—or my *Commentary* or *Partisan Review*—to an Italian coffee house on Bleecker Street for an espresso or, when it was warm enough, go down to Tompkins Square Park and read awhile on a favorite bench, read and look around and sometimes jot down a note about what I'd been writing that day, feeling very much the satisfactions of a young man on his own in a big city—to an ex-Newarker, a city far more mythical than Paris or Rome. If I wasn't as poor as those whose local park this was, I was still scrupulously living on the money that I portioned out to myself each week from the Houghton Mifflin fellowship; with no real desire to live otherwise, I felt perfectly at home loitering unnoticed among these immigrant Americans and their American offspring. I did not think of myself romantically as "one of them," it wasn't my style to speak of these people as The People, nor was I doing research—I knew plenty about old-country immigrants without having to study the sociology of Tompkins Square Park. I did think occasionally, however, of how my own family and all of our family friends had evolved from an immigrant existence that had to have shared at least certain elemental traits with the lives of the Tompkins Square Park regulars. I liked the place as much for its uneventful ordinariness as for the personal resonance that it had for me.

I don't intend to suggest that my sentimental fondness for Tompkins Square Park should have given Josie pause and sent her instead to look for her pregnant woman in Washington Square Park, only a ten-minute walk from my apartment in the other direction. To the contrary, had she gone anywhere *other* than Tompkins Square Park, she wouldn't have been the woman whose imagination's claim on my own may well have been what accounted for her inexplicable power over a supremely independent, self-assured, and enterprising young man, a stalwart competitor with a stubborn sense of determination and a strong desire to have his own way. The same deluded audacity that made even the least dramatic encounter promising, that had prompted her, probably quite spontaneously, to sign herself into the Chicago hospital as Jewish a mere hundred days into our affair, that had inspired her to hand over to my conventional, utterly respectable mother the dirty underthings that she'd accumulated on her holiday with me, was precisely what pointed her, like a hound dog with the sharpest nose for acerbic irony, to Tompkins Square Park in order to make a responsible man of me—to make a responsible *Jew* of me: to Tompkins Square Park, where she knew I so enjoyed my solitude and my pleasant sense of identification with my Americanized family's immigrant origins.

And a few days later, when she'd accepted my proposal to marry her—on the condition that before the marriage she have an abortion—it was the same instinct that led her to take the three hundred dollars I'd withdrawn from the bank and, instead of going with it to the abortionist whose name I had got from an intern friend, pocket the cash and spend the day in a movie theater in Times Square, repeatedly watching Susan Hayward go to the gas chamber in *I Want to Live!*

Yet once she'd "had" her abortion—after she'd come back from the movies to my basement apartment and, in tears, shivering uncontrollably, had told me from beneath the blankets on the bed all the horrible medical details of the humiliating procedure to which I had subjected her—why didn't I pick up *then* and run away, a free man? How could I *still* have stayed with her? The question really is how could I resist her. Look, how could I ever have resisted her? Forget the promise I'd made, after receiving the rabbit-test results, to make her my wife if only she got rid of the fetus—how could I be anything *but* mesmerized by this overbrimming talent for brazen self-invention, how could a half-formed, fledgling novelist hope ever to detach himself from this undiscourageable imagination unashamedly concocting the most diabolical ironies? It wasn't only she who wanted to be indissolubly joined to my authorship and my book but I who could not separate myself from hers.

I Want to Live!, a melodrama about a California B-girl who is framed for murder and goes to the gas chamber. The movie she went to see (instead of the abortionist, for whom she had no need) is also to be found in *My Life as a Man*. Why should I have tried to make up anything better? How could I? And for all I knew, Josie had herself made that up right on the spot, consulted her muse and blurted it out to me on the afternoon of her confession two years later . . . even, perhaps, as she invented on the spot—both to make her story more compelling and to torture me a little more—the urine specimen that she'd bought from the black woman in Tompkins Square Park. Maybe she did these things and maybe she didn't; she certainly did *something*—but who can distinguish what is so from what isn't so when confronted with a master of fabrication? The wanton scenes she improvised! The sheer hyperbole of what she imagined! The self-certainty unleashed by her own deceit! The conviction behind those caricatures!

It's no use pretending I didn't have a hand in nurturing

this talent. What may have begun as little more than a mendacious, provincial mentality tempted to ensnare a good catch was transformed, not by the weakness but by the strength of my resistance, into something marvelous and crazy, a bedazzling lunatic imagination that—everything else aside—rendered absolutely ridiculous my conventional university conceptions of fictional probability and all those elegant, Jamesian formulations I'd imbibed about proportion and indirection and tact. It took time and it took blood, and not, really, until I began *Portnoy's Complaint* would I be able to cut loose with anything approaching her gift for flabbergasting boldness. Without doubt she was my worst enemy ever, but, alas, she was also nothing less than the greatest creative-writing teacher of them all, specialist par excellence in the aesthetics of extremist fiction.

Reader, I married her.

All in the Family

I still don't think it was innocent of me to have been as astonished as I was at twenty-six when I found myself up against the most antagonistic social opposition of my life, and not from gentiles at one or the other end of the class spectrum but from angry middle-class and establishment Jews, and a number of eminent rabbis, accusing me of being anti-Semitic and self-hating. I hadn't begun to foresee this as a part of the struggle to write, and yet it was to be central to it.

As intellectually sophisticated as I was, "self-hatred" was still a new idea to me then; if the phenomenon had ever been present in my world, I had certainly never perceived it as a problem. In Newark, I hadn't known anyone to whose conduct self-hatred was anything like the key, and the Bucknell chapter of Sigma Alpha Mu, whatever its shortcomings, never seemed to chafe under its distinctive identity or noticeably to apologize for itself. When Moe Finkelstein, one of the

Sammies' two varsity football players, entered the game for Bucknell, his fraternity brothers invariably sent up a whoop signaling their proud affiliation, a demonstration of feeling that would have driven a self-hating Jew into paroxysms of shame. In fact, what was most admirable about the Sammies was the easygoing way in which they synthesized themselves into a manifestly gentile environment without denying their difference or combatively insisting on it. Theirs seemed to me, even then, a graceful response to a social situation that did not always bring out the best in people, particularly in that conformist era.

And virtually from the day that I arrived in Hyde Park as a graduate student and rented a tiny room in International House, the University of Chicago looked to me like some highly evolved, utopian extension of the Jewish world of my origins, as though the solidarity and intimate intensity of my old neighborhood life had been infused with a lifesaving appetite for intellectual amusement and experimentation. When I began graduate school in September 1954, the university seemed to me full of unmistakably Jewish Jews far *less* self-conscious and uncertain about themselves, really, than the Irish Catholics from Minnesota and the Baptists from Kansas—Jews wholly secularized but hardly chagrined by a pedigree from which they seemed to derive their undisguised contentiousness, their excitability, and a gift for satiric irony whose flavor I recognized immediately: our family friend Mickey Pasteelnik, Newark's Apple King, had he enjoyed a literary education, would surely have talked about *The Wings of the Dove* very much like my ebullient fellow student from Brooklyn, Arthur Geffin. Ted Solotaroff—with whom I profitably debated for years after I returned from the Army in 1956 and entered the Chicago Ph.D. program—remembers us referring to Isabel Archer as a "shiksa." I recall another conversation, over beer at the University Tavern, where Geffin tended bar at night, in which much scrupulosity was expended determining if Osmond wasn't really a Jew.

This was of course so much off-hours kibitzing, but the pleasure that we took in bringing to *The Portrait of a Lady* what we'd imbibed eavesdropping on our fathers' pinochle games does suggest something about the playful confidence we had in our Jewishness as an intellectual resource. It was also a defense against overrefinement, a counterweight to the intimidating power of Henry James and literary good taste generally, whose "civilizing" function was variously tempting to clever, ambitious city boys who knew just how casually coarse they could become on a street corner or at a poker game or in the upper deck at Ebbets Field. It seemed less advisable to treat this strain of vulgarity—which we had come to by being both our fathers' sons and our neighborhoods' creatures—as an impurity to be purged from our speech than to own up to it matter-of-factly, ironically, unashamedly, and to take a real, pleasurable satisfaction in what more than likely would have seemed to Henry James to be our unadventitious origins.

What ignited the Jewish charges against me was the publication in the *New Yorker*, in April 1959, of "Defender of the Faith," a story about some Jewish recruits in the wartime Army trying to extract favors from their reluctant Jewish sergeant. It was my second piece of fiction to appear in a large commercial magazine. With the $800 I'd earned from the first story, in *Esquire*, and an advance from Houghton Mifflin, I'd quit my instructorship at Chicago—and stepped for good (I thought) out of Josie's life. Intending to live only as a writer, I had moved to Manhattan's Lower East Side, to that two-room basement apartment that was placed perfectly—given my taste then for urban color—between the bums panhandling on the Bowery and the baskets of bialys on the tables at Ratners. The other stories about Jews that were to be published in the Houghton Mifflin collection, *Goodbye, Columbus*, though they may have attracted a little more than ordinary reader interest, had caused no furor among Jews, appearing as they did in the *Paris Review*, a young literary quarterly then with only a tiny circulation, and in *Commentary*, the monthly edited for years by Elliot Cohen and published by the American Jewish Committee. Had I submitted "Defender of the Faith" to *Commentary*—whose coeditor at that time, Martin Greenberg, was an early supporter and sympathetic friend—I suspect that the magazine would have published it and that the criticism the story aroused there would have been relatively unspectacular. It's even possible that the ferment inspired a month later by the publication of *Goodbye, Columbus*—the pulpit sermons, the household arguments, the discussions within Jewish organizations gauging my danger, all of which unexpectedly dramatized to people who were essentially nonreaders what was, after all, only a first book of short stories—might never have reached troublesome proportions had "Defender of the Faith" been certified as permissible Jewish discourse by appearing in *Commentary*. And had that happened—had there not been the inflammatory fanfare of the *New Yorker* exposure, had *Goodbye, Columbus* had the innocuous cultural fate of a minor critical success—it's likely that my alleged anti-Semitism might never have come to pervade the discussion of my work, stimulating me to defend myself in essays and public addresses and, when I decided to take things more aggressively in hand, to strike back at accusations that I had divulged Jewish secrets and vulgarly falsified Jewish lives by upping the ante in *Portnoy's Complaint*. *That* was not mistaken for a conciliatory act, and the ramifications of the uproar it fomented eventually inspired me to crystallize the public feud into the drama of internal family dissension that's the backbone of the Zuckerman series, which began to take shape some eight years later.

That the *New Yorker*, like *Partisan Review* and *Commentary*, had a Jewish editor, William Shawn, Jewish contributors—like S. J. Perelman, Irwin Shaw, Arthur Kober, and J. D. Salinger—and a sizable Jewish readership would only have suggested, to those I'd incensed, that identifying with the *New Yorker's* privileged, unequivocally non-Jewish aura furnished these Jews (as undoubtedly it did Roth himself) with far more sustenance than they derived from their Jewish status. I soon understood self-hatred to mean an internalized, though not necessarily conscious, loathing of one's recognizable group markings that culminates either in quasi-pathological efforts to expunge them or in the vicious disparagement of those who don't even know enough to try.

Because I didn't have the patience to wait for the author's copies to reach me by mail, the day that the *New Yorker* was scheduled to appear I made three trips to Fourteenth Street, to the newsstand across from Klein's, to see if the issue was in yet. When the magazine finally appeared that afternoon, I bought a copy for myself and another to send off to my parents. While I was at college, they had moved from the Weequahic neighborhood to a small garden apartment in a pleasant little complex in nearby Elizabeth, on the very street where they had been married in 1926 and where nearly every Sunday of my childhood, after visiting my widowed paternal grandmother in one of Newark's oldest immigrant neighborhoods, we would drive over to see my widowed maternal grandmother, who shared a small apartment there with my maiden aunt. The *New Yorker* was really no more familiar to my parents than were the other magazines in which my first stories had begun to appear. *Hygeia* had sometimes come to the house, sporadically we had received *Collier's*, *Liberty*, and the *Saturday Evening Post*, but the magazines to which my mother was most faithful were *Ladies' Home Journal*, *Redbook*, and *Woman's Home Companion*. In their pages she confirmed her sense of how to dress and to furnish a house, found the recipes that she clipped and filed in her recipe box, and received instruction in the current conventions of child rearing and marriage. Decorum and courtesy meant no less to her than they did to the heroines of the fiction she read in those magazines, and through her genteel example, my brother and I became well-mannered boys, always a source of pride to her, she said, on special Sunday outings to the Tavern, a family restaurant favored by Newark's Jewish bourgeoisie (a class in which we, who had neither money, property, nor very much social self-assurance, had really only half a foothold).

My mother read five or six books a year borrowed from the lending library, not junk but popular novels that had acquired moral prestige, like the works of Pearl Buck, her favorite author, whom she admired personally for the sort of reasons that she admired Sister Elizabeth Kenny, the esteemed Australian nurse who'd brought to America in the forties her therapeutic techniques for treating polio victims. She responded very strongly to their womanly brand of militant and challenging compassion. Her heroine of heroines was Eleanor Roosevelt, whose column, "My Day," she followed in the newspaper when she could. After her 1922 graduation from Battin High in Elizabeth, my mother, then Bess Finkel, had worked successfully for several years as an office secretary, a very dutiful daughter, living of course at home, who adored her mother and her older sister, feared her father, helped raise two younger sisters, and dearly loved her only brother,

Mickey—a musician as well as an art student, and eventually a quiet, unassuming bachelor, soft-spoken and witty, and something of a traveler. Artistic ambition moved him to paint portraits and landscapes but he kept himself alive doing professional photography; whenever he could afford to, he shut his tiny Philadelphia studio and sailed to Europe to tour the museums and look at the paintings he loved. Sandy and I were believed by my mother to derive our artistic proclivities through the genetic strain that had determined my Uncle Mickey's lonely career, and for all I know she was right. A woman of deep domestic expertise and benign unworldliness, reassuringly confident right up to the outermost boundaries of our social world though progressively, if respectably, uncertain anywhere beyond it, my mother was unambiguously proud of my first published stories. She had no idea that there could be anything seriously offensive about them and, when she came upon articles in the Jewish press intimating that I was a traitor, couldn't understand what my detractors were talking about. When she was once in doubt—having been shaken by a derogatory remark she'd overheard at a Hadassah meeting—she asked me if it could possibly be true that I was anti-Semitic, and when I smiled and shook my head no, she was entirely satisfied.

The issues of *Commentary* and the *Paris Review* that I'd sent in the mail or brought over with me to Elizabeth when I visited—containing my stories "Epstein," "Conversion of the Jews," and "You Can't Tell a Man by the Song He Sings"— my mother displayed, between bookends, on a side table in the living room. My father, who mainly read newspapers, was more aggressively exhibitionistic about my published works, showing the strange magazines to anyone who came to visit and even reading aloud to his friends lines in which he thought he recognized a detail of description, a name, a line of dialogue that I'd appropriated from a familiar source. After the publication of "Defender of the Faith," when I told him on the phone that the Anti-Defamation League of B'nai B'rith had requested I meet with their representatives to discuss the outcry over my story, he was incredulous. "What outcry? Everybody loved it. What is the outcry? I don't get it."

Perhaps if it had been somebody else's son against whom these accusations had been leveled by our Jewish betters, neither he nor my mother would have been quite so sure of the writer's probity, but for them to be wounded as Jews by *me*—whom they had seen circumcised and bar mitzvahed, whom they had sent for three years to one of our neighborhood's humble Hebrew schools, whose closest friends were all Jewish boys, who had always, unfailingly, been a source of pride—didn't occur to either of them and never would. My father could become as belligerent about the charges against my Jewish loyalty as he would be in later years when anyone dared to be dubious about a single aspect of Israeli policy.

I SHOULD ADD that not even he would have rushed to defend my achievements as a student of Judaism or my record of religious observance: at age thirteen I had not come away from three years of Hebrew School especially enlightened, nor had my sense of the sacred been much enriched. Though I hadn't been a total failure either, and had learned enough Hebrew to read at breakneck speed (if not with full comprehension) from the Torah at my bar mitzvah, the side of my Jewish education that had made that after-school hour, three days a week, at all endurable had largely to do with the hypnotic appeal, in those environs, of the unimpeachably profane. I am thinking of the witless persecution of poor Mr. Rosenblum, our refugee teacher, an escapee from Nazism, a man lucky (he had thought) just to be alive, whom the older boys more than once hung in effigy on the lamppost just outside the window where he was teaching our "four-to-five" class. I'm remembering the alarming decrepitude of the old-country *shammes*, our herring-eater, Mr. Fox, whom we drove crazy playing a kind of sidewalk handball called "Aces Up" against the rear wall of his synagogue—Mr. Fox, who used to raid the local candy store and pull teenagers at the pinball machine out by the neck in order to scare up enough souls for a *minyan*. And, of course, I'm remembering the mishap of a nine-year-old classmate, a boy of excruciating timidity, who on our very first day of Hebrew School in 1943—when the rabbi who was religious leader of the synagogue and director of the school began, a bit orotundly, to address us new students in our cubbyhole classroom directly upstairs from the Ark of the Covenant—involuntarily beshat himself, a pathetic disaster that struck the nervous class as blasphemously hilarious.

In those after-school hours at the dingy Hebrew School—when I would have given anything to have been outdoors playing ball until suppertime—I sensed underlying everything a turbulence that I didn't at all associate with the airy, orderly public school where I was a bright American boy from nine to three, a bubbling, energetic unruliness that conflicted head-on with all the exacting ritual laws that I was now being asked to obey devoutly. In the clash between the anguished solemnity communicated to us by the mysterious bee-buzz of synagogue prayer and the irreverence implicit in the spirit of animated mischievousness that manifested itself almost daily in the little upstairs classrooms of the *shul*, I recognized something far more "Jewish" than I ever did in the never-never-land stories of Jewish tents in Jewish deserts inhabited by Jews conspicuously lacking local last names like Ginsky, Nusbaum, and Strulowitz. Despite everything that we Jews couldn't eat—except at the Chinese restaurant, where the pork came stowed away in the egg roll, and at the Jersey shore, where the clams skulked unseen in the depths of the chowder—despite all our taboos and prohibitions and our vaunted self-denial, a nervous forcefulness decidedly *irrepressible* pulsated through our daily life, converting even the agonizing annoyance of having to go to Hebrew School, when you could have been "up the field" playing left end or first base, into unpredictably paradoxical theater.

What I still can recall from my Hebrew School education is that whatever else it may have been for my generation to grow up Jewish in America, it was usually entertaining. I don't think that an English Jewish child would necessarily have felt that way and, of course, for millions of Jewish children east of England, to grow up Jewish was tragic. And that we seemed to understand without even needing to be told.

Not only did growing up Jewish in Newark in the thirties and forties, Hebrew School and all, feel like a perfectly legitimate way of growing up American but, what's more, growing up Jewish as I did and growing up American seemed to me indistinguishable. Remember that in those days there was not a new Jewish country, a "homeland," to foster the range of attachments—the pride, the love, the anxiety, the chauvinism, the philanthropy, the chagrin, the shame—that have, for many American Jews now over forty, complicated anew the issue of Jewish self-definition. Nor was there quite the nostalgia for the old Jewish country that Broadway later began to merchandise with the sentimentalizing of Sholom Aleichem. We knew very well that our grandparents had not torn themselves away from their shtetl families, had not left behind parents whom they would never see again, because back home everybody had gone around the village singing show tunes that brought tears to your eyes. They'd left because life was awful; so awful, in fact, so menacing or impoverished or hope-lessly obstructed, that it was best forgotten. The willful am-nesia that I generally came up against whenever I tried as a child to establish the details of our pre-American existence was not unique to our family.

I would think that much of the exuberance with which I and others of my generation of Jewish children seized our opportunities after the war—that wonderful feeling that one was entitled to no less than anyone else, that one could do anything and could be excluded from nothing—came from our belief in the boundlessness of the democracy in which we lived and to which we belonged. It's hard to imagine that anyone of intelligence growing up in America since the Viet-nam War can have had our unambiguous sense, as young adolescents immediately after the victory over Nazi fascism and Japanese militarism, of belonging to the greatest nation on earth.

AT MY LUNCH MEETING about "Defender of the Faith" with two representatives from the Anti-Defamation League, I said that being interviewed by them as an alleged purveyor of material harmful and defamatory to the Jews was particularly disorienting since, as a high school senior thinking about studying law, I had sometimes imagined working on their staff, defending the civil and legal rights of Jews. In response, there was neither chastisement nor accusation and nothing resembling a warning about what I should write or where I should publish. They told me that they had wanted to meet me only to let me know about the complaints they had re-ceived and to answer any questions I might have. I figured, however, that a part of their mission was also to see whether I was a nut, and in the atmosphere of easygoing civility that had been established among us over lunch, I said as much, and we all laughed. I asked who exactly they thought the people were who'd called in and written, and the three of us speculated as to what in the story had been most provocative and why. We parted as amicably as we'd met, and I only heard from the ADL again a couple of years later, when I was invited by their Chicago branch to participate in an interfaith symposium, cosponsored by Loyola University, on the "image" of Catholics and Jews in American literature.

After *Goodbye, Columbus* won the 1960 National Book Award for Fiction and the Daroff Award of the Jewish Book Council of America, I was asked to speak on similar themes before college Hillel groups, Jewish community centers, and temples all over the country. (I was on a Guggenheim in Rome in 1960 and unable to be present for the Daroff Award ceremony in New York. My strongest supporter on the prize jury, the late critic and teacher David Boroff, confirmed the report I got from my friend Bob Silvers—who had been there to accept the award on my behalf—which was that my book had been an unpopular choice, with the sponsors as well as with many gathered together for the ceremony; the year before, another set of judges had given the prize to Leon Uris for *Exodus*.) When I could get away from university teaching, I took up these invitations and appeared before Jewish audiences to talk and to answer questions. The audiences were respectfully polite, if at times aloof, and the hostile members generally held their fire until the question period had begun. I was up to the give-and-take of these exchanges, though I never looked forward to them. I'd had no intention as a writer of coming to be known as "controversial" and, in the beginning, had no idea that my stories would prove repugnant to ordinary Jews. I had thought of myself as something of an authority on ordinary Jewish life, with its penchant for self-satire and hyperbolic comedy, and for a long time continued to be as bemused privately as I was unyielding publicly when confronted by Jewish challengers.

In 1962, I accepted an invitation to appear on a panel at Yeshiva University in New York. I felt it a duty to respond to the pronounced Jewish interest my book continued to evoke and I particularly didn't want to shy away from such an obvious Jewish stronghold; as one of the panel participants would be Ralph Ellison, I was also flattered to have been asked to speak from the same platform. The third panelist was Pietro di Donato, a relatively obscure writer since the success in the thirties of his proletariat novel *Christ in Concrete*.

From the start I was suspicious of the flat-out assertiveness of the Yeshiva symposium title—"The Crisis of Conscience in Minority Writers of Fiction"—and its presumption, as I interpreted it, that the chief cause of dissension over "minority" literature lay not in the social uncertainties of a minority audience but in a profound disturbance in the moral faculties of minority writers. Though I had no real understanding of seriously observant Jews—a group nearly as foreign to me as the devoutest Catholics—I knew enough not to expect such people, who would comprise most of the Yeshiva faculty and student body, to be supporters of my cause. But since the discussion would be held in a university auditorium—and I was very much at home in such places—and inasmuch as I had been invited not to address a narrowly Jewish subject on my own but to investigate the general situation of the minority writer in America with an Italian-American writer whom I was curious to meet and a highly esteemed black writer of whom I was in awe, I didn't foresee just how demoralizing the confrontation could be.

I came East from Iowa with Josie, and on the evening of the symposium the two of us took a taxi out to Yeshiva with

my new Random House editor, Joe Fox, who was eager to
hear the discussion. Random House was publishing *Letting
Go,* my second book, later in the year, but as *Goodbye, Columbus* had been published by Houghton Mifflin, Joe had had
no direct involvement with those inflammatory stories and,
as a gentile, was removed from the controversy and perplexed
by its origins. Josie was, of course, gentile also, but after our
marriage, on her own steam—and against my better judgment, not to mention my secular convictions—she had taken
religious instruction from Rabbi Jack Cohen at the Recon-
structionist Synagogue in Manhattan and been converted by
him to Judaism. We were first married in a civil ceremony—
with only two friends for witnesses—by a justice of the peace
in Yonkers; several months later Jack Cohen married us again,
at his synagogue, in a religious ceremony attended by my
parents. The second ceremony struck me—and perhaps struck
my parents, who were too bewildered, however, to be anything but polite—as not only unnecessary but, in the circumstances, vulgar and ludicrous. I participated so that her
pointless conversion might at least appear to have some util-
itarian value, though my consent didn't mean that it wasn't
distressingly clear to me that this was one more misguided
attempt to manufacture a marital bond where the mismatch
was blatant and already catastrophic. To me, being a Jew had
to do with a real historical predicament into which you were
born and not with some identity you chose to don after reading
a dozen books. I could as easily have turned into a subject of
the Crown by presenting my master's degree in English literature to Winston Churchill as my new wife could become
a Jew by studying with Jack Cohen, sensible and dedicated
as he was, for the rest of her life.

I saw in her desire to be some sort of simulated Jew yet
another distressing collapse of integrity; something very like

the self-hatred with which I had been stigmatized seemed to impel her drive to camouflage the markings of her own small-town, Middle Western past by falsifying again her affiliation with me and my background. I introduce this story not so as to have one more go at Josie but to reveal a bizarre irony of which I was not unconscious while the spanking-new Jew of unmistakable Nordic appearance sat in the Yeshiva audience looking on at the "excommunication" of the Semitic-featured young writer whose seventeen years as his parents' child in the Weequahic neighborhood couldn't have left him more inextinguishably Jewish.

The trial (in every sense) began after di Donato, Ellison, and I had each delivered twenty-minute introductory statements. Ellison rambled on easily and intelligently from a few notes, di Donato winged it not very logically, and I read from some prepared pages, thus allowing me to speak confidently while guarding, I thought, against an interrogator's altering the context in which my argument was being made; I was determined to take every precaution against being misunderstood. When the moderator began the second stage of the symposium by questioning us about our opening statements, the only panelist he seemed truly interested in was me. His first question, following di Donato's monologue—which would have seemed, had I been moderating, to require rigorous clarification—was this: "Mr. Roth, would you write the same stories you've written if you were living in Nazi Germany?"— a question that was to turn up some twenty years later in *The Ghost Writer*, asked of Nathan Zuckerman by Judge Leopold Wapter.

Thirty minutes later, I was still being grilled. No response I gave was satisfactory and, when the audience was allowed to take up the challenge, I realized that I was not just opposed but hated. I've never forgotten my addled reaction: an un-

dertow of bodily fatigue took hold and began sweeping me
away from that auditorium even as I tried to reply coherently
to one denunciation after another (for we had by then proceeded beyond interrogation to anathema). My combative instinct, which was not undeveloped, simply withered away and
I had actually to suppress a desire to close my eyes and, in
my chair at the panelists' table, with an open microphone only
inches from my perspiring face, drift into unconsciousness.
Ralph Ellison must have noticed my tenacity fading because
all at once I heard him defending me with an eloquent authority that I could never have hoped to muster from halfway
out to oblivion. His intellectual position was virtually identical
to mine, but he was presenting it as a black American, in-
structing through examples drawn from *Invisible Man* and the
ambiguous relationship that novel had established with some
vocal members of his own race. His remarks seemed to appear
to the audience far more creditable than mine or perhaps
situated the audience so far from its real mission as to deflate
or deflect the inquisitorial pressure that I had envisioned
mounting toward a finale that would find me either stoned to
death or fast asleep.

With me relegated pretty much to the sidelines, the evening shortly came to an end. From the moderator there were
genial good wishes for the panelists, from the spectators there
was some scattered applause, and then we all started down
off the stage by the side stairs leading into the house. I was
immediately surrounded by the element in the audience most
antagonistic to my work, whom Ellison's intercession had
clearly curtailed only temporarily. The climax of the tribunal
was upon me, and though I was now wide awake, I still
couldn't extricate myself that easily from their midst. Standing
in the well between the hall and the stage, with Joe and Josie
visible beyond the faces of my jury—though in no conceivable

way my Jewry—I listened to the final verdict against me, as harsh a judgment as I ever hope to hear in this or any other world. I only began to shout "Clear away, step back—I'm getting out of here" after somebody, shaking a fist in my face, began to holler, "You were brought up on anti-Semitic literature!" "Yes," I hollered back, "and what is that?"—curious really to know what he meant. "English literature!" he cried. "English literature is anti-Semitic literature!"

In midtown Manhattan later, Josie, Joe, and I went to have something to eat at the Stage Delicatessen, down the street from the hotel where we were staying. I was angry at what I had stupidly let myself in for, I was wretchedly ashamed of my performance, and I was infuriated still by the accusations from the floor. Over my pastrami sandwich no less, I said, "I'll never write about Jews again." Equally ridiculously, I thought that I meant it, or at least that I should. I couldn't see then, fresh from the event, that the most bruising public exchange of my life constituted not the end of my imagination's involvement with the Jews, let alone an excommunication, but the real beginning of my thralldom. I had assumed—mostly from the evidence of *Letting Go*—that I had passed beyond the concerns of my collection of apprentice stories and the subjects that had fallen so naturally to me as a beginning writer. *Letting Go*, about the unanticipated responsibilities of young adulthood far from Jewish New Jersey, seemed to foreshadow the direction in which new preoccupations would now guide me. But the Yeshiva battle, instead of putting me off Jewish fictional subjects for good, demonstrated as nothing had before the full force of aggressive rage that made the issue of Jewish self-definition and Jewish allegiance so inflammatory. This group whose embrace once had offered me so much security was itself fanatically insecure. How could I conclude otherwise when I was told that every word I wrote was a disgrace, potentially endangering every Jew? Fanatical security, fanatical insecurity—nothing in my entire background could exemplify better than that night did how deeply rooted the Jewish drama was in this duality.

After an experience like mine at Yeshiva, a writer would have had to be no writer at all to go looking elsewhere for something to write about. My humiliation before the Yeshiva belligerents—indeed, the angry Jewish resistance that I aroused virtually from the start—was the luckiest break I could have had. I was branded.

Now Vee May Perhaps to Begin

The summer house that May Aldridge and I rented was on a quiet blacktop road in the center of Martha's Vineyard, a few minutes' walk from the general store in West Tisbury. It was a small, undistinguished house, comfortable enough, though with the exception of the double bed furnished almost exclusively with faded old beach chairs. The windows were bare when we moved up from New York in late June of 1967, and May drove to the cut-rate store in Vineyard Haven and bought fabric to make curtains. An independent woman of thirty-four whose substantial income derived from a family trust fund, she really didn't have to sit down and sew curtains together out of inexpensive yard goods in order to make ends meet; but at the time I was hardly rich, and we were sharing the house on the assumption that we'd live in it as though we were two people with the same modest means. May managed this simply enough, not only because of her accommodating character (or because we were in love), but because the challenge of her adult life had been to loosen the inhibiting bond between herself and the manner to which she'd been born, in which she was rooted, and by which she'd been left distressingly vulnerable, with too little confidence in her good, clear mind, and unable to animate in a sustained way the passionately felt side of an obliging nature.

May was a gentile woman at the other end of the American spectrum from Josie. She had been sent off to the best schools by an old-line Cleveland paint-manufacturing family that had achieved enormous financial success, as well as the civic distinction and social prominence that once came automatically to American industrial clans of British stock. Fair and green-eyed and slender, she was the loveliest-looking woman I'd ever known, her beauty as delicate as Josie's attractiveness, when we'd first met, was stolidly earthbound. It was an appearance as indelibly stamped by privilege as Josie's had been by her provincial small town. The two women were drastically different physical types from social backgrounds that couldn't have been much more dissimilar and, as women, so unlike as to seem like representatives of divergent genders. In each, inborn character proclivities appeared to have been carried to a stereotypical extreme by something innately disabling in their social origins, so that where Josie, the daughter of a working-class loser, was blunt, scrappy, dissatisfied, envious, resentful, and schemingly opportunistic, May for many years had camouflaged her uncertainties behind a finishing-school facade of nearly self-suffocating decorum. What they shared were the scars of wounds inflicted by the social mentality governing their upbringing; what had drawn me to them (and, more than likely, them to me) was not that they were members in good standing of their respective bloodlines, solidly entrenched in the world of their fathers, but that they were intriguingly estranged from the very strata of American society of which they were each such distinctively emblazoned offspring.

During our five years together, May never once suggested that we go out to Cleveland to meet her family, and when her mother visited her every few months in New York, instead of following our usual routine of my joining May for the evening and sleeping overnight at her East Seventy-eighth Street apartment, I would stay at my own place in Kips Bay, which I'd come to use—on the days when I wasn't away teaching university classes in Philadelphia or Stony Brook—as little more than a writing studio. Of course we understood that it wasn't just our unmarried state but also my being a Jew that had something to do with why meeting her parents was probably just as well avoided. Neither of us expected anything horrendous to result from the encounter—we simply didn't see any reason, so long as we *were* single, to create unnecessary tensions with a family living hundreds of miles away, who themselves seemed more than willing to steer clear of their daughter's intimate life. My curiosity about May's Cleveland background couldn't begin to match my desire to keep the affair from becoming entangled with family concerns; I'd had enough of that.

I did invite my own parents over from New Jersey one evening to have a drink at May's apartment and to go out with us for dinner. I wanted them to witness how, with May, my life had been restored and simplified; though they'd never known exactly how lurid my marriage had been, they'd had plenty of intimations, had seen the toll it had taken on me, and, as a result, had suffered terribly. My mother, who was so reassured by good manners and herself socially so proper, found May's graciousness tremendously appealing and would have been only too happy if, on the spot, May could have magically replaced Josie, to whom it seemed I'd been eternally bonded by the State of New York. Though my father also happened to like May, I think he would have been relieved had I taken up with a kangaroo. After my separation from Josie in 1962, she had traveled down to his office in south Jersey and, in lieu of the alimony payments that she claimed I was failing to make, demanded money from him. When my father told her, correctly, that I *was* meeting my legal obligations, she berated *him* for *his* irresponsibility.

May's uptown apartment was large and comfortably furnished without being studiously decorated or at all pretentious; that her possessions, however, reflected so clearly the traditional tastes of her class suggested that she'd always remain interlinked with her origins in a thousand telling ways, regardless of how willingly she allied herself with the social style of my New York friends, most of whom were Jews from backgrounds not unlike my own. As for her friends—people she'd known for years and had sometimes helped with their interior decorating—after a few nights out with them, I had had to tell her that, affable as it all was, those evenings weren't for me. It turned out that she was herself a little weary of them too, and one day, after lots of encouragement from me, she decided to quit decorating and redecorating those Upper East Side apartments and enrolled at Hunter to finish her undergraduate education; it had been interrupted in 1952, when she'd suffered an emotional crisis at Smith and, at twenty, had returned home to Cleveland to take up, unhappily, a protected, innocuous postdebutante life. Much as I wanted to help her get herself going as a new woman, I had no desire for her to ape Josie and renounce what she was or cut the ties to where she was from, however unwelcome or uneasy I might have found myself there, and especially as what still interested us both lay precisely in the *unlikeliness* of our connection.

Though slow to develop because of the sexual wariness that each of us had developed late in our twenties, our earnest physical fervor became in time a source of almost mystifying comfort and happiness. In May's nudity there was something at once furtive and shy that aroused a kind of tender hunger that I couldn't remember having felt for years. Hers was the body of a sweet-tempered woman who, in her remotest dreams, could never have feigned pregnancy or intentionally allowed herself to become impregnated in order to foster a scenario to which she was pathologically addicted: to make of herself the helpless female victim and of the man the heartless victimizer. There was no strategy in May's desire; had there been, she wouldn't have been quite so outfoxed, as she was in college and again later when she came from Cleveland to live alone in New York, by the wily exploiters of trusting girls. For me, the guilelessness that could be construed in the lines of her body as easily as in her gaze seemed to offer a powerful assurance of integrity, and it was from this that my frazzled virility took heart and my regeneration began.

MAY AND I HAD COME TO RENT houses on Martha's Vineyard two summers running because of my friendship with Robert Brustein, who was then teaching drama at Columbia and writing theater reviews for the *New Republic*. Bob and his wife, Norma, lived during the year in a big apartment on the Upper East Side of Manhattan, where I'd often gone for dinner when I was new to New York and on my own. It was at the Brusteins' dinner table that I began to find an appreciative audience for a kind of noisy comedy, and the sort of Jewish subject, that wasn't like anything in *When She Was Good*, the book I was writing about Lucy Nelson of Liberty Center, U.S.A. The spirit of my next book, *Portnoy's Complaint*, began to materialize as entertainment for Bob and Norma and for the friends of theirs who became my friends, city Jews of my generation, analysands with deep parental attachments, respectable professionals unimpeded by the gentility principle and with a well-developed taste for farcical improvisation, particularly for recycling into boisterous comic mythology the communal values by which our irreducible Jewishness had been shaped. It was an audience I'd lost touch with since I'd left Chicago and begun married life with Josie in Rome, London, Iowa City, and Princeton—an audience knowledgeable enough to discern, even in the minutest detail, where reportage ended and Dada began and to enjoy the ambiguous overlap. Unembarrassed by unrefined Jewish origins, matter-of-factly confident of equal American status, they felt American *through* their families' immigrant experiences rather than in spite of them and delighted in the shameless airing of extravagant routines concocted from the life we had all grown up with.

Far from causing us to feel at the periphery of American society, the origins that had so strongly marked our style of self-expression seemed to have placed us at the heart of the city's abrasive, hypercritical, potentially explosive cultural atmosphere as it was evolving out of the angry response to the Vietnam War. Lyndon Johnson, betraying every foreign-policy position by which he'd been sharply distinguished from Barry Goldwater in the 1964 election campaign, had, in only two years, made himself the natural target for a brand of contempt that had never, in my lifetime, been vented with such vehement imagination and on such a scale against a figure of such great authority. His own outsized personality seemed, paradoxically, to be the fountainhead for that steamrolling defiance that his politics would come to generate in many of those repelled by the war. There was something boisterous and unconstrainable in him, the potential in his very physique for a kind of mastodon rage, that made him the inspirational impresario as much for the ugly extremes of theatrical combat dividing the society as for the Southeast Asia conflict. To me it always seemed that his was the hateful, looming, uncontrollable presence that, at least initially, had activated the fantastical style of obscene satire that began to challenge virtually every hallowed rule of social propriety in the middle and late sixties.

What I found, then, in New York, after leaving my wife and moving up from Princeton—where, for as long as I remained on the university faculty, Josie continued to make her home—were the ingredients that inspired *Portnoy's Complaint*, whose publication in 1969 determined every important choice I made during the next decade. There was this audience of sympathetic Jewish friends who responded with euphoric recognition to my dinner-table narratives; there was my intense psychoanalysis, which, undertaken to stitch back together the confidence shredded to bits in my marriage, itself became a model for reckless narrative disclosure of a kind I hadn't learned from Henry James; there was May, a trustworthy, exceedingly tender woman in dire need herself of affectionate attention, with whom a mutual convalescence, grounded in demidomesticity, proceeded at a steady, invigorating pace; and there was May's unequivocal gentileness, bestowed by her upbringing and revealed by genetic markings that made her as unimpeachably Aryan as I was Jewish, and that it wouldn't have entered her mind to attempt, like Josie, to disguise or renounce. There was, in other words, a pervasive anthropological dimension to our love affair that delineated just the sort of tribal difference that would empower Portnoy's manic self-presentation.

Lastly, there was the ferocity of the rebellious rhetoric unleashed against the president and his war, the assault that

Johnson's own seething cornball bravado inspired and from which even he, with his rich and randy vein of linguistic contempt, had eventually to flee in defeat, as though before a deluge of verbal napalm. It bedazzled me, this enraged invective so potent as to wound to the quick a colossus like Lyndon Johnson, especially after my long, unnatural interlude of personal and literary self-subjugation.

I WAS THIRTY-FOUR in the autumn following that second, splendidly healing Vineyard summer with May and so never quite grasped how close to death I had come, not even when, having begun to feel some strength returning, I asked the surgeon how much more of the fall I was going to miss, cooped up in the hospital. He answered, with a bemused smile, "Don't you get it *yet*? You almost missed everything." I heard his words, I never forgot his words, and yet the experience registered not as my having nearly died but instead as my having met with death and overcome it. I felt as though now I needn't worry about dying for another thousand years.

Amazingly, I didn't see my burst appendix as Josie's handiwork, probably because the poisons of peritonitis spread through my system without her accompanying barrage of moral indictment. It was a separate ordeal entirely, the denouement of a decade that had posed somewhat preposterous tests of strength, but arising clearly out of a family predisposition toward which it was a relief not to feel a personal antagonism. What had killed two of my uncles, and very nearly, in 1944, killed my father, had tried and failed to kill me. This was the sort of ordeal whose lucky outcome heightens tremendously your respect for the place of chance in an individual destiny; once the cozy part of the convalescence begins, you float buoyantly off on feelings of sentimental kinship with virtually everyone else fortunate enough to have been left living. My life with Josie, by contrast, had isolated me as a case, bizarrely cut off in a bad marriage that wasn't merely bad in its own way but included among its hazards the oft-repeated threat of murder. I felt strong and lucky, like a human being among human beings, for having survived peritonitis; I would never know what to make of myself for having endured and survived my wife, though not for lack of thinking about it. For years afterward I was to think and brood and fictionalize obsessively about how I had made Josie happen to me. And it's become apparent, while writing this, that I'm all too capable of thinking about it still.

Every evening at dinnertime May came to the hospital to see me; during the day she had her Hunter classes and also worked part-time as a draft counselor with a Quaker group in Murray Hill, advising draft-age young men about the alternatives to military service. The job was hardly congenial to her temperament, but the war had mobilized her indignation in an unforeseen way. She was not the only American discovering in herself the power to oppose; however, as someone for whom taking the public steps that counted one among the opposition did not come easily, she wasn't overjoyed by what conviction sometimes demanded of her, such as having to phone the Cleveland banker who oversaw her trust fund and requesting of that ultraconservative gentleman and family friend that her portfolio be divested of "war stocks" like Dow Chemical. It was irresistible, of course, for her old Manhattan friends to see in this transformation of a polite, retiring society heiress nothing more "political" than the overbearing influence of me and *my* friends. And it's true that on her own, in her old world, May Aldridge might not have turned spontaneously into a dedicated antiwar worker; nonetheless, it wasn't really any position of mine that influenced her so much as the confidence inspired by the affair itself, generating in her a belief that she (who had been stuck so long in what had felt like an unalterable existence gathering swatches for other people's upholstery) could hope to help change, right along with her own fate, the American war policy. Because she was being stirred into action on virtually every front, the last traces of self-protective meekness largely disappeared, and something touchingly animated and akin to the furtiveness that I found so stirring in her nudity turned her characteristic placidity into genuine composure, with a power and effectiveness of its own.

A month after my emergency appendectomy I was released from the hospital and then, two weeks later, unexpectedly readmitted, this time for the removal of the stump of the blown appendix, which had failed to atrophy and had become infected. It was to be another thirty days before I came out for good, as thin as I'd been as a junior in high school but healthy at last. With May I went down to a tiny island off the west coast of Florida to recuperate for a couple of weeks. We stopped off to have lunch in Miami Beach, where my parents were wintering in an apartment they'd taken in the same complex as some of their old Newark friends, and then in a rented car we drove across to Fort Myers and out over the causeway to Captiva. There wasn't much to do there: we strolled the beaches with the elderly people who were out collecting shells, there were pelicans to watch, dolphins swam by, and a couple of mornings we went to the bird sanctuary with our lunch and followed the cormorants with field glasses. I was bored and edgy a lot of the time, impatient now with the enforced idleness of an extended bout of ill health and eager to get back to writing. A new book was well under way, and I was afraid of losing the galloping pace that had got me going. A section entitled "Whacking Off" had appeared in

Partisan Review; Ted Solotaroff, who'd just begun *New American Review*, had featured another section in his first issue and wanted to publish more; and my Random House editors, Joe Fox and Jason Epstein, had read a rough first draft and told me I was on to something. I wanted to get back to work, Ted wanted me to get back to work, Jason and Joe wanted me to get back to work, but probably nobody wanted me to get back and finish what I'd begun quite as much as Josie: the rumor in New York publishing circles—and Josie was working finally at a publishing job—was that my new novel, if it was anything like what Solotaroff, Epstein, and Fox were saying, would command a large advance.

BY THE TIME I'd fallen ill in the autumn of 1967, the worst of my separation seemed to be over. It was five years since I'd left Josie, and though she still refused to divorce me and planned to take me back to court in the new year to try for a second time to get the alimony of $125 a week increased, I had not seen her outside a courtroom, and it was a long while since she'd telephoned during the day to tell me how wicked I was or in the middle of the night, generally after too much drink, to announce, "You're in bed with some Negress!" When I moved from Princeton to Manhattan, after finally leaving her in the last weeks of 1962, she followed suit some eight months later; she hoped to resume the plan interrupted by our marriage—to work in publishing—while simultaneously she wanted me to support her, a goal best pursued in the state where I was domiciled and where antiquated divorce laws made it likely that, if she continued to prefer it that way, I would legally remain her husband forever.

She could also better keep track of my whereabouts in New York than she could back in Chicago, close to where her two children were now in boarding schools, supported by the aunt and uncle of her first husband. For instance, one night when Helen, her twelve-year-old daughter, came East during a vacation to visit her mother, I arranged to take the girl to dinner and to the theater. While we waited in our seats for the play to begin, I was served from the aisle with a subpoena. I immediately recognized the polite gentleman who was serving me; previously he had served me politely while I was at the dentist's. Pretending to Helen that the envelope I'd been handed was something that I was expecting to be delivered at the theater, I thanked him and slipped it into my jacket pocket. During the intermission, while Helen was in the lobby having an orange drink, I went to the men's room, where, in a stall, I opened the envelope and read the subpoena. I could barely contain my fury. The subpoena, summoning me to court to face another alimony challenge, could have been served on me in my apartment any day of the week: I had a university teaching job and, after months in a New York sublet, I clearly wasn't about to skip town. Nonetheless, Josie had arranged to have me served while I was out entertaining Helen, as though her daughter hadn't been sufficiently scarred by all the sexual battling she'd seen and as though my own capacity to show the child a good time might not be strained by an unanticipated announcement of yet another resumption of our conflict.

During the year that Helen had lived with us in Iowa City, where I was teaching in the Writers' Workshop of the state university, I'd served as a surrogate father. Helen was alarmingly needy but also very engaging, and taking serious parental responsibility for her wasn't simply a burden. Her pathetic difficulties with her studies required lots of attention, but she was a little girl quick to smile and genial with our best friends, and it could be fun to take her to the Iowa football games or to ice skate with her on the river or, with her help, to rake the leaves from the lawn in the fall. Josie was pleased when Helen and I began to grow close, but as the months went by and family life became routinized, there were also astonishing outbursts to throw a lurid shadow over this too. A sudden tirade about the probity of men would end with a warning that if ever I laid a finger on her ten-year-old daughter she would drive a knife into my heart. One evening, following a bedroom argument culminating in just such a threat, I waited until everyone had fallen asleep and then rounded up all the kitchen knives and locked them in the trunk of the car. Early the next morning, when Helen was alone in the kitchen making herself some breakfast, I came down in my robe to find her looking mightily perturbed. "What's the matter?" I asked her. "It's getting to be late for school! I have to cut my grape-fruit and I can't find a knife!" I went out to the garage and got her one.

By 1967, then, I was still saddled with alimony amounting to about half my income; my lawyer led me to understand that the alimony could be expected to increase proportionally with any substantial increase in my income and that I would be paying it for the rest of my life, unless Josie one day remarried. To me the alimony was court-ordered robbery and never more galling to pay than when I remembered, while making out the check, how the brief marriage had come to be in the first place. That was a story I couldn't forget. I couldn't forget it because I was the fall guy but also because the urine story was one of the best stories I'd ever heard. Had I been a dermatologist or an engineer or a shoemaker, after five years there might have been little more than the alimony left to dwell on; but what obsessed me no less than what was being taken from me was the story that she'd bestowed on me—for a man in my business it was too good to give up.

Actually, *When She Was Good* was intended to have provided me with a setting for that urine story, but after several fragmentary, unsatisfactory drafts, it veered away from this purpose and ended up as an imaginary elaboration, at once freely invented and yet close to the spirit—and even to the pattern of events—of the legend of her upbringing, her adolescence, and her first marriage as it had been narrated to me over the kitchen table throughout our early months as lovers in Chicago.

Between 1959 and 1962, during several week-long visits to her home in Port Safehold, a small Michigan resort town on the eastern shore of the lake, I'd got to know some of the main characters in Josie's tale. Port Safehold could have been Bombay, so strong was its hold on me—and this, long before I thought that an environment like it could ever provide the backdrop for a story of mine; what made me so curious was that it was the backdrop for the grim saga of gentile family suffering that was hers. I was a guest of her maternal grandfather, Merle Hebert—known to relatives as Daddy Merle—in the very room where Josie had grown up after her family, whom her father could never really support, had moved in with the Heberts. Sitting out on the front porch with Daddy Merle after supper, I'd get him to talking about the old days and, though he was a gentle, decorous fellow, a retired carpenter and simple small-towner claiming proudly to bear no one a grudge, when I asked about Smoky Jensen he had to admit that his son-in-law had been something of a disappointment. Josie's mother was living then in a little apartment near the commercial crossroads of the town, not far from the local newspaper where she worked as the advertising manager. She seemed more worldly and self-sufficient than the woman Josie had described to me as her father's defenseless victim, and we quickly developed a friendship. When I came to write

When She Was Good, however, I discounted my observations and, following Josie's narrative lead—which she'd instinctively decided was more damning all around and which certainly made everything harsher and dramatically more vivid—I imagined, as the affronted young heroine's mother, a childish, daughterly woman totally *un*defended against her irresponsible husband.

Eventually the book became for me a time machine through which to look backward and discover the origins of that deranged hypermorality to whose demands I had proved so hopelessly accessible in my early twenties. I was trying to come to some understanding of this destructive force, but separate from my own ordeal, to exorcise her power over me by taking it back to its local origins and tracing in detail the formative history of injury and disappointment right on down to its grisly consequences—again, not as they'd erupted in the context of our marriage (I was fighting too hard to be free of our marriage to spare the energy for that) but as they might have evolved had she been, instead of a Josie who'd escaped her past at least geographically and had wound up a working woman in Hyde Park, a Lucy imprisoned in the enraging, emotionally overcharged hometown with its full roster, for her, of betrayers, cowards, and vicious enemies. I was ridding myself in *When She Was Good* of the narrative spell that her legend had so successfully cast over my will, a purgation achieved by taking the victim's gruesome story as gospel, but then enlarging it with a hard-won, belated understanding of the inner deformation suffered by the victim herself—perhaps suffered even more grotesquely than anything else and ending inescapably in her self-destruction.

Lucy's hideous death at the end of *When She Was Good* was neither wishful thinking nor authorial retribution. I simply didn't see how the disintegration of someone so relentlessly exercised over the most fundamental human claims, so enemy-ridden and unforgivingly defiant, could lead, in that little town, to anything other than the madhouse or the grave.

IN APRIL 1968 I was virtually the only customer eating an early dinner at Ballato's Restaurant on Houston Street when the news came over the radio that Martin Luther King had been shot. The owner, my friend the late John Ballato, a courtly gentleman, Sicilian-born and at one time a syndicalist in New York's Little Italy, brought his fist down violently on the table where we had been sitting and talking together. "Those sons of bitches!" John said angrily, his eyes filling with tears. "Those dogs!" I went to the phone and called May, who was working late at the Quaker Center. We agreed to meet back at her apartment, where we later sat up on the bed together and watched again and again the TV footage from Memphis, which never stopped being terrible or true no matter how many times it was played. I phoned friends. I phoned my father. "Newark's going to go up," he said, "you'll see." He said it several times and of course he was right. Watching the television clips of King's great public moments, May sporadically began to cry. I didn't—for all his force, King, whom I had never met, had always struck me as personally remote, almost featureless, his moral self-conception on the scale of a mountain rather than of a man, and so what his death provoked in me wasn't tears of pity and grief but a sense of foreboding and fear: an unspeakable crime was going to cause unimaginable social disaster.

When Bobby Kennedy was assassinated a few months later, May and I were up watching the aftermath of the California primary and so learned he'd been shot only seconds after it happened. I had signed ads in behalf of Eugene McCarthy's candidacy for the Democratic presidential nomination and been to a few meetings and gatherings backing his candidacy, but the previous summer May and I had nonetheless enjoyed enormously a dinner with Kennedy on Martha's Vineyard, at the house of his speechwriter, Dick Goodwin, who'd become a Vineyard acquaintance. Kennedy was crackling that evening with energy and charm, perhaps having the best time of the ten of us at the table. He was clearly getting a kick out of flirtatiously quizzing May, who was seated beside him, about her Cleveland society background; at the close of the dinner, he said to her in a voice deliberately loud enough for me to overhear, "And is Mr. Roth going to marry you?" May smiled and said, "That remains to be seen." "Mr. Roth," he said, flashing at me that smile of his as distinctive as Franklin Roosevelt's and weighted with a similar bravado, "do you intend to marry this woman?" "It depends, Senator, if I can ever get a divorce in your state from the wife I'm already married to." "And," Kennedy replied, "you'd like me to look into that— is that it?" "I wouldn't say no. I don't have to tell you I could make it worth your while." Whereupon Senator Kennedy, happily puffing on his cigar, turned to one of his legislative aides and told him to find out about getting a divorce for Mr. Roth so that he could marry Miss Aldridge as soon as possible.

He was by no means a political figure constructed on anything other than the human scale, and so, the night of his assassination and for days afterward, one felt witness to the violent cutting down not of a monumental force for justice and social change like King or the powerful embodiment of a people's massive misfortunes or a titan of religious potency but rather of a rival—of a vital, imperfect, high-strung, egotistical, rivalrous, talented brother, who could be just as nasty as he was decent. The murder of a boyish politician of forty-two, a man so nakedly ambitious and virile, was a crime against ordinary human hope as well as against the claims of robust, independent appetite and, coming after the murders of President Kennedy at forty-six and Martin Luther King at thirty-nine, evoked the simplest, most familiar forms of despair.

Between the assassinations of Martin Luther King and Bobby Kennedy, Josie too was violently killed. Death came instantly, in the early hours of a May morning, when the car in which she was being driven across Central Park left the road and struck a tree, a lamppost, or a concrete abutment—nobody who spoke to me seemed to know precisely how or where the collision took place. The driver was an editor who had been Josie's boss at her publishing job until, as I was led to understand, he had recently fired her. The fact that he was black made me remember those accusing calls I would get from her in the middle of the night, after I'd moved up from Princeton to a New York hotel, when she'd contend drunkenly that I was with a "Negress"—made me remember them without, however, leading me to understand her any better. I remembered that the pregnant woman from whom she'd bought the urine specimen was black as well—could she be the "Negress" Josie would imagine me with in my New York bed? Only the gods of Paranoia knew the answer to that.

The editor had escaped serious injury and appeared at the funeral wearing a small Band-Aid over one eye but still looking dazed and shaken. We merely shook hands when we were introduced; I figured it was best to display no curiosity about the car crash, since a number of Josie's mourners—members of her therapy group who knew the history of my sadism inside out—must already have been wondering if I hadn't somehow been an accomplice to it. Nor did the editor, either then or later, give any indication of wanting to talk to me about the circumstances of the accident. In fact, after shaking his hand at the funeral—and despite his having been cast as the instrument to tear asunder my eternal marriage and extinguish every last responsibility that she and the State of New York claimed to be mine—I never saw, or heard of, my emancipator again.

It would have been ridiculous for me to have thought that in *When She Was Good* I had divined Josie's death, which took place in entirely different circumstances from Lucy Nelson's and resulted from an accident in which her will did not figure, whereas Lucy's own enraged decision leads to her freezing to death in the snow. And yet, a year after the publication of *When She Was Good*, when I got the news that she was dead, I was transfixed at first by the uncanny overlapping of the book's ending with the actual event. I also found it hard to believe that Josie's will *hadn't* figured in the accident, probably because I had never forgotten how, in the midst of an argument en route from Italy to France in the late spring of 1960, she had furiously tried to take the wheel and kill us both while I was driving north through the mountains in our little Renault. However, if the real circumstances had indeed "validated" the fatal destiny of that personification of Josie's defiant extremism which I presented as Lucy Nelson, I would never know. And what difference would knowing have made anyway?

Josie's daughter had by this time left her Chicago-area boarding school and, at seventeen, come to live with Josie in New York, where she was attending a public high school and where, for *her* outspoken antiwar sentiments, she had come to be known, according to a friend of mine who lived on their street, as Hanoi Helen. It was she who called me at my apartment early on Saturday morning, as I was sitting down to work after returning from May's. Like Peter Tarnopol in an all but identical situation in *My Life as a Man*, I didn't believe her when she said that Josie was dead. I had already been deceived by my wife more than once, and though it was almost impossible to envision Helen—with whom my relationship was still affectionate, though now more avuncular than anxiously paternal—acting wittingly as Josie's coconspirator in a hoax so grotesque, my immediate response was total disbelief: it was a trick, I thought, to get me to say something self-incriminating that could be recorded and used to sway the judge to increase the alimony in our next court go-round. I also didn't believe then that miracles happen, that one's worst enemy, who one has hoped and prayed would disappear from one's life, could suddenly be eradicated in a car accident, and in, of all places, Central Park, where May and I, along with tens of thousands of others, were only recently demonstrators against the war and where the two of us took our long Sunday walks. All I had done the night before was to close my eyes and go to sleep, and now everything was over. Who could be naïve enough to buy that? It would have been only slightly more incredible (if aesthetically symmetrical) had I learned that she'd been bludgeoned to death in Tompkins Square Park on the very spot where the urine purchase had been negotiated nine years earlier.

I asked Helen to repeat for me slowly what she had just said. When she did—"Mother's dead"—I said skeptically, "And where is she now?" Her response was graphic enough to stun me out of my self-protecting incredulity. "In the morgue," she said, and began to cry. "You have to identify her, Philip—I can't!" Within minutes I was down at the apartment in the West Twenties, where Helen was being kept company by one of Josie's close friends. Scattered around the apartment, which, of course, I'd never seen before, were all sorts of familiar things that we had accumulated in our marriage, most of them inexpensive little art objects that we'd brought back from Italy after our year there on my Guggenheim. I couldn't take my eyes off the shelves of books—there had been a highly emotional dispute in front of the judge about whose books were whose, after which, in accord with his wisdom, the secondhand Modern Library novels that I'd purchased as a graduate student for twenty-five cents apiece were divided evenly between us. I'd forgotten about them (almost) until I recognized a couple of my books on her living-room shelves, and once again, despite the presence of Josie's friend and Helen's obvious distress, I felt as though some trick was being played, madly excessive, ghoulish perhaps, but in the face of which I had better watch every word I said. I was in a state akin to shock and persisted in believing that she wasn't dead at all, that, if anything, she was kneeling behind the door to the next room, along with her lawyer and maybe even the judge. *See how he's enjoying this, Your Honor? It's just as we've told you—his heart is flint!*

How could she be dead if I didn't do it?

Helen asked again if I would go to the morgue. I said I didn't see where it was my place to identify the body, there were plenty of people to do that other than her or me; if she wished, however, I would make the funeral arrangements. Only a little later I was on my way to Frank Campbell's Funeral Chapel on Madison and Eighty-first Street. In those days I didn't casually ride taxis in New York and, in fact, was walking over to catch a subway uptown when I realized that there was no need to economize in quite the way I did only the day before, when she and I were dividing my income. That was the first tangible result of my no longer being married to her—I could take a taxi to the funeral home to bury her.

The ride from the West Twenties on a Saturday morning didn't take more than ten or so minutes. Outside Campbell's door, when I went to pay the driver, he turned around and smiled at me: "Got the good news early, huh?" I was flab-

bergasted by what he'd said and afterward could only conclude
that all the way up in the taxi I, the son of a family of irrepressible whistlers, must have been whistling away—how else
could he have known?

Helen had told me that Josie had instructed her that when
she died she wanted a Jewish funeral service, and so a Jewish
funeral service she got. There was a certain sweetness to be
found in sitting alongside the rabbi in the funeral director's
office, deciding on the appropriate psalms for him to read,
especially as he turned out to be (for reasons no more fath-
omable than anything else about her leaving this life while
there was still litigation to attend to) one of the New York
rabbis on record as considering me a menace to the Jews. I
didn't go so far as to wear a yarmulke at the service, but had
the rabbi asked me to, I would have forsworn my secular
convictions out of respect for the beliefs of the deceased.
When I saw the casket, I said to Josie, "You're dead and I
didn't have to do it." Whereupon the late Jew replied, "Mazel
tov." That is, I replied on her behalf. And I did because she'd
never reply to me again and I'd never have to reply to her or
to a subpoena of hers—that is, outside of fiction. She was
dead, I hadn't done it, but it would still take years of hapless
experimentation before I could decontaminate myself of my
rage and discover how to expropriate the hatred of her as an
objective subject rather than be driven by it as the motive
dictating everything. *My Life as a Man* would turn out to be
far less my revenge on her than, given the unyielding problems it presented, hers on me. Writing it consisted of making
one false start after another and, over the years it took to finish
it, very nearly broke my will. The only experience worse than
writing it, however, would have been for me to have endured
that marriage without afterward having been able to find ways
of reimagining it into a fiction with a persuasive existence
independent of myself.

Actually, if it hadn't been for residual feelings of responsibility to Helen and her brother, Donald—who by then was an eighteen-year-old high school senior in a Chicago boarding school and who had flown in from Chicago with his father and his father's aunt to attend the funeral—I would have considered it grossly inappropriate to turn up for the service at Campbell's, let alone to seem to want to suggest to anyone there that my heart was anything *other* than flint. I felt precisely like what she'd been telling me I was since the first time we'd broken up in Chicago in 1956: her ineradicable need for a conscienceless, compassionless monster as a mate had at last been realized—I felt absolutely nothing about her dying at thirty-nine other than immeasurable relief.

Helen and Donald sat between me and their father, a small-town radio-station engineer whom Josie had begun dating as a high school girl when he'd come back home from the service in the mid-forties. Though he was altogether civil at the funeral, he certainly had no reason to like me much, since it was I, exuding impassioned moral zeal, who had taken off after him in the courts when Josie and I returned from Rome in the fall of 1960 and found that her two children, who were supposed to have been domiciled with her ex-husband and his new wife, were living with him alone in a southern Illinois suburban development, the new wife apparently having taken leave of him while we were abroad. The plan that evolved to alter this arrangement, and that finally required the court to implement, was for Josie to recover partial custody of the children, for Donald to board at a private school (toward whose costs I would contribute something), and for Helen to come to live with us in Iowa City, where I had taken a university teaching job in the Writers' Workshop.

I had thrown myself with all my energy—and my small cash reserves—into the court battle that ensued, frequently phoning and writing our Chicago lawyer to go over details of the case and doing what I could on holidays and weekends, when the children visited Iowa City, to gain their confidence about the new plans for them, to which their father continued to have strenuous objections. We were also setting the stage for them to spend the summer with us in Amagansett, Long Island. I thought not only that these arrangements would be better for Helen and Donald, who had fallen way behind in school and were now about to witness yet another marital breakup, but that seeing to their welfare might somehow mitigate Josie's relentless desperation. It was the sort of rescue operation that, however difficult, can grow naturally enough out of a strong and harmonious marriage; in a marriage like ours, beyond reclamation before it had even begun, the pathetic needs of her unhappy children simply furnished a means of remobilizing the forces that had crazily joined us in the first place. My disastrously confused, unaccountable sense of personal obligation was once again activated by the wreckage of her chaotic emotional past.

In 1975, a journalist for a Jewish community newspaper in a Midwestern city discovered that my "stepson"—as Donald was misleadingly described in the longish article "Papa Portnoy: Philip Roth as a Stepfather"—was a young married truck driver living in a local working-class neighborhood. Donald came off in the piece as a lively, unashamed young fellow, interested in social problems and possessed of the direct, congenial openness you associate with a good community organizer, a job that in fact he filled in his spare time. Donald recalled accurately for the interviewer that our relationship had been both affable and relentlessly pedagogical—as he described it, a "positive" one: "I've got to say that if it were not for the positive influence Philip had on my life at that time, I might be in jail today." He remembered that I had given him books to read, that I'd tutored him one summer

for his school entrance exams, and that I also had taught him
a little elementary European history after he'd quite innocently delivered himself of some childish, if to me grating,
misinformation about the relationship of the Nazis to the Jews
in World War II. His sole significant memory lapse had to do
with Josie's funeral: he told the reporter—when the reporter
asked—that I hadn't been there.

In fact, I was just a seat away from him and, the morning
after the funeral, took Donald by himself to breakfast at the
old Biltmore Hotel, where we talked about his college plans.
He flew back home with his father that day, and I never saw
him again, until, that is, the inquisitive journalist sent me his
published interview with Portnoy's stepson, offering me, in
an accompanying letter, the opportunity in his paper "to express yourself on the issues raised in the article." There, along
with photographs reprinted from the New York *Daily News*,
of Josie and me at the New York Supreme Court building
during the separation proceedings in 1964, was a photograph
of Donald in his late twenties, mustached, wearing a cap, and
seated at the wheel of his pickup truck.

After breakfast with Donald, before returning to my Kips
Bay apartment—and to the point in my manuscript where I'd
been interrupted by Helen's call—I walked over to Central
Park and tried to find the spot where the car was said to have
crashed and killed her. It was a splendid spring morning and
I sat on the grass nearby for about an hour, my head raised
to take the sun full in my face. Like it or not, that's what I
did: gloried in the sunshine on my living flesh. "She died and
you didn't," and that to me summed it up. I'd always understood that one of us would have to die for the damn thing
ever to be over.

Only a few days after her funeral I made arrangements,
virtually overnight, to be a guest at Yaddo, the Saratoga

Springs artists' colony where I'd frequently gone off to write
for long stretches between semesters and during the summer,
especially before I'd met May, when I was newly returned to
Manhattan, alone in a garish sublet apartment, dealing with
the alimony battle and barely able to concentrate on anything
else. The bus from Port Authority Terminal was for me very
much a part of the stealthy, satisfying ritual of leaving Manhattan for the safe haven of Yaddo, and so instead of renting
a car, which would have been more in keeping with my new
relaxed attitude toward taking a New York cab, I showed up
at the bus station in my old clothes and boarded the north-
bound Adirondack bus, rereading on the long trip up the
thruway the rough first draft of the last two chapters of my
book. At Yaddo, where there were only seven or eight other
guests in residence, I found that my imagination was fully
fired: I worked steadily in a secluded hillside cabin for twelve
and fourteen hours a day until the book was done, and then
I took the bus back down, feeling triumphant and indestructible.

The Roth family menace, peritonitis, had failed to kill me,
Josie was dead and I didn't do it, and a fourth book, unlike
any I'd written before in both its exuberance and its design,
had been completed in a burst of hard work. What had begun
as a hopped-up, semifalsified version of an analytic monologue
that might have been mine, by diverging more and more from
mine through its mounting hyperbole and the oddly legendary
status conferred by farcical invention upon the unholy trinity
of father, mother, and Jewish son, had gradually been transformed into a full-scale comical counteranalysis. Unhampered
by fealty to real events and people, it was more entertaining,
more graphic, and more shapely than my own analysis, if not
quite to the point of my personal difficulties. It was a book
that had rather less to do with "freeing" me from my Jewish-

ness or from my family (the purpose divined by many, who were convinced by the evidence of *Portnoy's Complaint* that the author had to be on bad terms with both) than with liberating me from an apprentice's literary models, particularly from the awesome graduate-school authority of Henry James, whose *Portrait of a Lady* had been a virtual handbook during the early drafts of *Letting Go*, and from the example of Flaubert, whose detached irony in the face of a small-town woman's disastrous delusions had me obsessively thumbing through the pages of *Madame Bovary* during the years I was searching for the perch from which to observe the people in *When She Was Good*.

In my Yaddo cabin I gave the babbling book's last word to the desperately clowning analysand's silent psychoanalyst. The single line was intended not only to place a dubious seal of authority on the undecorous, un-Jamesian narrative liberties but to have a secondary, more personal irony for me as both hopeful instruction and congratulatory message: "So [said the doctor], now vee may perhaps to begin. Yes?"

When I returned to Manhattan, Candida Donadio, who was my literary agent then, got on the phone with my publisher, Bennett Cerf, the president of Random House, and in a matter of hours we had all agreed on the terms of a contract guaranteeing me an advance of $250,000. After paying ten percent to Candida and (sweating heavily as I wrote out the checks) giving another seventy percent to my accountant for quarterly tax payments to New York City, New York State, and the IRS, I still had a new balance in my account that was about a hundred times larger than any I'd ever had there in my life. By the next day I had dashed off checks to pay my debts of some $8,000 and had also purchased two first-class tickets on the *France*, luxury-liner passage to England for May and me; we planned to sublet a London flat for the summer and drive from there to see the English cathedrals and countryside. May told me that I would need a tuxedo to eat my caviar on the ship, and so we went down to pre-chic Barneys on Seventeenth Street and I bought one. She smiled when I tried it on; half meaning it, she said, "I could take you back to Cleveland in that." "Sure," I said, "we'd wow 'em at the country club. Especially after my little book comes out." That was the first and the last I ever heard about taking me back to Cleveland.

The crossing was an enjoyable masquerade, to which even the ship's magazine contributed by publishing a photograph of May and me in our evening clothes, identified as "Mr. and Mrs. Philip Roth." Only when we disembarked and made our way up to London and a suite at the Ritz, from which we began apartment hunting, did the restlessness begin. At my first meeting with an attractive young English journalist whom my English publisher had arranged to have interview me, I offered an invitation, which she gracefully declined, to spend the rest of the afternoon with me in a hotel. I proceeded to have clothes made by three distinguished tailoring establishments, half a dozen suits that I didn't need, that required endless, stupefying fittings, and that finally never fit me anyway. We went on trips to famously quaint villages, we hunted out the oldest Anglo-Saxon churches, we made love before a huge bedroom mirror in our rented flat, and what I saw in the mirror held no more of my attention than did the quaint villages and antique churches. On English TV I watched Mayor Daley's police surging through the Chicago streets in pursuit of yippies and other conventioneers, and wondered what the hell I was doing trying vainly to have a good time abroad while the turbulence of the American sixties, which had enlivened both my fiction and my life, looked finally to be boiling over. I wandered down Curzon Street with nothing to do one morning and found myself a Chinese call girl; then May and I headed off to see Salisbury Cathedral, but only after I'd stopped on my way out of London at Dougie Hayward's exclusive tailoring shop to have a pair of suit trousers refitted that were still fashionably too tight in the crotch.

Perhaps if May and I had gone back and rented the modest house on the back roads of Martha's Vineyard and, within the confines of that pleasant, familiar island, among dear friends, let the massive changes trickle slowly in, I wouldn't have had to experience so pointlessly *my* turbulence, the upheavals of someone who feels himself all but reborn. An extravagant blowout on the *France* or at the Ritz, an hour at the Hilton with a petite Hong Kong pro, however symbolically appropriate and pleasurable in passing, had nothing much to do with the potential for personal resurrection that seemed to be promised by the astonishing annihilation of my nemesis, the violent dissolution of the enshackling marriage, and the imminent publication, on a grandish scale, of a book imprinted with a style and a subject that were, at last, distinctively my own. All I did that summer in England was to nick ridiculously away at the carapace of strictures that had kept me resolved and persevering during the years in which I'd impotently raged against Josie's exactions and, through an enervating process of trial and error, tracked my unexploited resources as a novelist.

By the time we'd returned to America in September, I had decided to live completely on my own. Now that it was possible in the late Senator Kennedy's state for me to marry May (or anyone else I chose), the idea was intolerable: I was not about to be reined in right off by, of all things, another marriage certificate. That May, inside a marriage or out, hadn't the slightest potential for behaving like Josie wasn't even the point; I simply could not unlearn overnight what the years of legal battling had taught me, which was never, but *never*, to hand over again to the state and its judiciary the power to decide to whom I should be most profoundly committed, in what way, and for how long. I could not imagine ever again being a husband who was ultimately under their punitive mechanisms of authority, and, however little I may have experienced of genuine fatherhood as a part-time pedagogue helping Josie's children learn their ABCs, I felt that I could not be a father under their jurisdiction either. The subpoenas, the depositions, the courtroom inquisitions, the property disputes, the newspaper coverage, the legal bills—it had all been too painful and too humiliating and had gone on far too long for me ever again voluntarily to become the plaything of those moral imbeciles. What's more, I now didn't even wish to be bound by what had been the countervailing balm to the legacy of marital hatred, the loving loyalty of May Aldridge. Instead I was determined to be an absolutely independent, self-sufficient man—to recapture, in other words, twelve years on, at age thirty-five, that exhilarating, adventurous sense of personal freedom that had prompted the high-flying freshman-composition teacher, on a fall evening in 1956, to go blithely forward in his new Brooks Brothers suit and, without the slightest idea that he might be risking his life, handily pick up on a Chicago street the small-town blond divorcée with the two little fatherless children, the penniless ex-waitress whom he'd already spotted serving cheeseburgers back in graduate school, and who'd looked to him like nothing so much as the All-American girl, albeit one enticingly at odds with her origins.

Dear Roth,

I've read the manuscript twice. Here is the candor you ask for: Don't publish—you are far better off writing about me than "accurately" reporting your own life. Could it be that you've turned yourself into a subject not only because you're tired of me but because you believe I am no longer someone through whom you can detach yourself from your biography at the same time that you exploit its crises, themes, tensions, and surprises? Well, on the evidence of what I've just read, I'd say you're still as much in need of me as I of you—and that I need you is indisputable. For me to speak of "my" anything would be ridiculous, however much there has been established in me the illusion of an independent existence. I owe everything to you, while you, however, owe me nothing less than the freedom to write freely. I am your permission, your indiscretion, the key to disclosure. I understand that now as I never did before.

What you choose to tell in fiction is different from what you're permitted to tell when nothing's being fictionalized, and in this book you are not permitted to tell what it is you tell best: kind, discreet, careful—changing people's names because you're worried about hurting their feelings—no, this isn't you at your most interesting. In the fiction you can be so much more truthful without worrying all the time about causing direct pain. You try to pass off here as frankness what looks to me like the dance of the seven veils—what's on the page is like a code for something missing. Inhibition appears not only as a reluctance to say certain things but, equally disappointing, as a slowing of pace, a refusal to explode, a relinquishing of the need I ordinarily associate with you for the acute, explosive moment.

As for characterization, you, Roth, are the least completely rendered of all your protagonists. Your gift is not to personalize your experience but to personify it, to embody it in the representation of a person who is *not* yourself. You are not an autobiographer, you're a personificator. You have the reverse experience of most of your American contemporaries. Your acquaintance with the facts, your sense of the facts, is much less developed than your understanding, your intuitive weighing and balancing of fiction. You make a fictional world that is far more exciting than the world it comes out of. My guess is that you've written metamorphoses of yourself so many times, you no longer have any idea what *you* are or ever were. By now what you are is a walking text.

The history of your education as narrated here—of going out into the world, leaving the small circle, and getting your head knocked in—certainly doesn't strike me as more dense or eventful than my own as narrated in my bildungsroman, excepting, of course, for the marital ordeal. You point out that something like that experience would eventually become the fate of my unfortunate predecessor, Tarnopol; for this I can't be sufficiently grateful, though when it came to the Jewish opposition to my writing, I only wish that, like yours, my own occupation would not have pitted me against my family.

I wonder if you have any real idea of what it's like to be disowned by a dying father because of something you wrote. I assure you that there is no equivalence between that and a *hundred* nights on the rack at Yeshiva. My father's condemnation of me provided you, obviously, with the opportunity to pull out all the stops on a Jewish deathbed scene; that had to have been irresistible to a temperament like yours. Nonetheless, knowing what I now do about your father's enthusiasm for your first stories and about the pride he took in their publication, I feel, whether inappropriately or not, envious, cheated, and misused. Wouldn't you? Wouldn't you at least be mildly disturbed to learn, say, that Josie had been inflicted on you for artistic reasons, that the justification for your misery stemmed solely from the requirements of a novel that wasn't even your own? You'd be furious, more furious even than you were when you thought she'd landed on you out of the blue.

But I'm fixed forever as what you've made me—among other things, as a young writer without parental support. Whether you ever were what you claim to have been is another matter and requires some investigating. What one chooses to reveal in fiction is governed by a motive fundamentally aesthetic; we judge the author of a novel by how well he or she tells the story. But we judge morally the author of an autobiography, whose governing motive is primarily ethical as against aesthetic. How close is the narration to the truth? Is the author hiding his or her motives, presenting his or her actions and thoughts to lay bare the essential nature of conditions or trying to hide something, telling in order *not* to tell? In a way we always tell in order also not to tell, but the personal historian is expected to resist to the utmost the ordinary impulse to falsify, distort, and deny. Is this really "you" or is it what you want to look like to your readers at the age of fifty-five? You tell me in your letter that the book feels like the first thing you have ever written "unconsciously." Do you mean that *The Facts* is an unconscious work of fiction? Are you not aware yourself of its fiction-making tricks? Think of the exclusions, the selective nature of it, the very pose of fact-facer. Is all this manipulation truly unconscious or is it pretending to be unconscious?

I think I am able to understand the plan here despite my opposition to your publishing the book. In somewhat autonomous essays, each about a different area in which you pushed against something, you're remembering those forces in your early life that have given your fiction its character and also reflecting on the relationship between what happens in a life and what happens when you write about it—how close to life it sometimes is and how far from life it sometimes is. You see your writing as evolving out of three things. First, there's your journey from Weequahic Jewishness into the bigger American society. This business of being able to be an American was always problematic for your parents' generation, and you sensed the difference between yourself and those who had preceded you—a difference that wouldn't have been a factor in the artistic evolution of, say, a young James Jones. You developed all the self-consciousness of someone confronted with the choices of rising up out of an ethnic group. That sense of being part of America merges in all sorts of ways with your personality. Second, there was the terrific upheaval of the involvement with Josie and the self-consciousness this ignited about your inner weaknesses as a man. Third, as far as I can make it out, there's your response to the larger world, beginning with your boyhood awareness of World War II, Metropolitan Life, and gentile Newark and culminating in the turbulence of the sixties in New York, particularly the outcry there against the Vietnam War. The whole book seems to be leading to the point where these three forces in your life intersect, producing *Portnoy's Complaint*. You break out of a series of safe circles—home, neighborhood, fraternity, Bucknell—you manage even to shake off the spell of the great Gayle Milman, to discover what a life is like "away." You show us where away is, all right, but what's driving you there you keep largely to yourself, because you either don't know or cannot talk about it without me as your front man.

It's as if you had worked out in your mind the formula for who you are, and this is it. Very neat—but where's the struggle, the *struggling* you? Maybe it *was* easy to get from Leslie Street to Newark Rutgers to Bucknell to Chicago, to leave the Jewish identification behind in a religious sense but retain it in an ethnic sense, to be drawn into the possibilities of goy America and feel that you have all the freedom that anyone else has. It's one of the classic stories of twentieth-century American energy—out of an ethnic family and then made by school. But I still feel that you're not telling all that's going on. Because if there wasn't a struggle, then it just doesn't seem like Philip Roth to me. It could be anybody, almost.

There's an awful lot of loving gentleness in those opening chapters of yours, a tone of reconciliation that strikes me as suspiciously unsubstantiated and so unlike what you usually do. At one point I thought the book should be called *Goodbye Letting Go Being Good*. Are we to believe that this warm, comforting home portrayed there is the home that nurtured the author of *Portnoy's Complaint*? Strange lack of logic in that, but then creation is not logical. Could I honestly tell you that I dislike the prologue? A subdued and honorable and respectful tribute to a striving, conscientious, determined father—how can I be against that? Or against the fact that you find yourself bowled over, at the verge of tears with your feelings for this eighty-six-year-old man. This is the incredible drama that nearly all of us encounter in relation to our families. The gallantry and misery of your father as he approaches death has so tenderized you, so opened you up, that *all* these recollections seem to flow from that source. And as for the final paragraph about your animal love for your mother? Quite beautiful. Your Jewish readers are finally going to glean from this what they've wanted to hear from you for three decades. That your parents had a good son who loved them. And what's no less laudable, what goes hand in hand with the confession of filial love, is that instead of writing only about Jews at one another's throats, you have discovered gentile anti-Semitism, and are exposing *that* for a change.

Of course, all that's been there and apparent right along, even if not to them; but what they need is just this, your separating the facts from the imagination and emptying them of their potential dramatic energy. But why suppress the imagination that's served you so long? Doing so entails terrific discipline, I know, but why bother? Especially when to strip away the imagination to get to a fiction's factual basis is frequently all that many readers really care about anyway. Why is it that when they talk about the facts they feel they're on more solid ground than when they talk about the fiction? The truth is that the facts are much more refractory and unmanageable and inconclusive, and can actually kill the very sort of inquiry that imagination opens up. Your work has always been to intertwine the facts *with* the imagination, but here you're unintertwining them, you're pulling them apart, you're peeling the skin off your imagination, *de*-imagining a life's work, and what is left even they can now understand. Thirty years ago, the "good" boy is thought of as bad and thereby given enormous freedom to *be* bad; now, when the same people read those opening sections, the bad boy is going to be perceived as good, and you will be given the kindliest reception. Well, maybe that'll convince you better than I ever could to go back to being bad; it should.

Of course, by projecting essentially fictional characters with manic personae out into the world, you openly invited misunderstanding about yourself. But because some people get it wrong and don't have any idea of who or what you really are doesn't suggest to me that you have to straighten them out. Just the opposite—consider having tricked them into those beliefs a *success*; that's what fiction's *supposed* to do. The way things stand you're no worse off than most people, who, as you know, often are to be heard mumbling aloud, "Nobody understands me or knows my great worth—nobody knows what I'm really like underneath!" For a novelist, that predicament is to be cherished. All you need as a writer is to be loved and forgiven by all the people who have been telling you for years to clean up your act—if there's anything that can put the kibosh on a literary career, it's the loving forgiveness of one's natural enemies. Let them keep reminding their friends not to read you—you just keep coming back at them with your imagination, and give up on giving them, thirty years too late, the speech of the good boy at the synagogue. The whole point about your fiction (and in America, not only yours) is that the imagination is always in transit between the good boy *and* the bad boy—that's the tension that leads to revelation.

Speaking of being loved, just look at how you begin this thing. The little marsupial in his mother's sealskin pouch. No wonder you suddenly display a secret passion to be universally coddled. But where, by the way, is the mother after that? It may well be that this incredible animal love that you have for your mother, and that you allude to in only one sentence in the prologue, can't be exposed by you undisguised, but aside from that sealskin coat, there is no mother. Of course it speaks volumes, that coat—it tells nearly everything you need to know about your mother at that point; but the fact remains that your mother has no developed role either in your life or in your father's. This picture of your mother is a way of saying "I was not my mother's Alexander nor was she my Sophie Portnoy." Perhaps that's true. Yet this image of an utterly refined, Jewish Florence Nightingale still seems to me particularly striking for all it appears to omit.

Nor have I any idea what's going on with you in relation to your father, his rise in the world, his fall in the world, his rise again. There's only a sense of you and Newark, you and America, you and Bucknell, but what is going on within you and within the family is not here, can't be here, simply because it *is* you and not Tarnopol, Kepesh, Portnoy, or me. In the few comments you do make about your mother and father, there's nothing but tenderness, respect, understanding, all those wonderful emotions that I, for one, have come to distrust partly because you, for one, have made me distrust them. Many people don't like you as a writer just because of the ways you invite the reader to distrust those very sentiments that you now publicly embrace. Comfort yourself, if you like, with the thought that this is Zuckerman talking, the disowned son embittered permanently by his deprivation; take solace in that if you like, but the fact remains I'm not a fool and I don't believe you. Look, this place you come from does not produce artists so much as it produces dentists and accountants. I'm convinced that there is something in the romance of your childhood that you're not permitting yourself to talk about, though without it the rest of the book makes no sense. I just cannot trust you as a memoirist the way I trust you as a novelist because, as I've said, to tell what you tell best is forbidden to you here by a decorous, citizenly, filial conscience. With this book you've tied your hands behind your back and tried to write it with your toes.

You see your beginnings, up to and including Bucknell, as an idyll, a pastoral, allowing little if no room for inner turmoil, the discovery in yourself of a dark, or unruly, or untamed side. Again, this may be dismissed as so much Zuckermania, but I don't buy it. Your psychoanalysis you present in barely more than a sentence. I wonder why. Don't you remember, or are the themes too embarrassing? I'm not saying you *are* Portnoy any more than I'm saying you are me or I am Carnovsky; but come on, what did you and the doctor talk about for seven years—the camaraderie up at the playground among all you harmless little Jewish boys? In fact, after the prologue and those first two sections, I can see the hero becoming a lawyer, a doctor, a suburban developer—he's had his literary fling, his maverick fun, he's had his gentile Polly, and now he's going to settle down, marry into a good Jewish family, make money, be rich, have three children—and you have Josie instead. So there's something missing, a big gap—those idyllic sections don't at all add up to "Girl of My Dreams." The very end of the little prologue, lyrically evoking the fleshly bond to your mother, tell me, please, how do you get from that to Josie? As you yourself point out, Josie isn't something that merely happened to you, she's something *that you made happen*. But if that is so, I want to know what it is that led to her from that easy, wonderful, shockless childhood that you describe, what it is that led to her from the cozily combative afternoons with Pete and Dick at Miss Martin's seminar. Your story in Newark and Lewisburg was far from tragic—

and then, in an extraordinarily brief period, you became im-
mersed in the pathologically tragic. Why? Why did you essentially mortify yourself in a passionate encounter with a
woman who had a sign on her saying STAY AWAY KEEP OUT?
There has to be some natural link between the beginning,
between all that early easy success, culminating at Bucknell
and Chicago, and the end, and there isn't. Because what's
left out is the motive.

   In the exploits with Polly, the encounter with Mrs. Nellenback, the business with *The Bucknellian*, there's no sense
that you're truly dissatisfied and looking for something else.
Only glancingly do you touch on your dissatisfactions; even
the conflict with your father you treat peripherally, and yet
the note of grievance, of criticism, of disgust and satire and
estrangement, sounds so powerfully in your fiction. Which
am I to believe is the posturing: the fiction or this? Everything
you describe in your childhood is undoubtedly still strongly
there—the well-brought-up side, the nice-guy side, the good-
kid side. This manuscript is steeped in the nice-guy side. In
autobiography you seem to have no choice but to document
mainly the nice-guy side, the form signaling to you that it is
probably wisest to suppress the free exploration of just about
everything else that goes into the making of a human personality. Where once there was satiric rebellion, now there is a
deep sense of belonging; no resentment but rather gratitude,
gratitude even for crazy Josie, gratitude even for the enraged
Jews and the wound they inflicted. Of course, you are not the
first novelist who, by fleeing the wearying demands of fictional
invention for a little vacation in straightforward recollection,
has shackled the less sociable impulses that led him or her to
become a novelist in the first place. But the fact remains that
it wasn't exactly the nice-guy side that got the Yeshiva people
all hot under their tefillin. And what you *were* tapping there

did not come from nothing, even if it looks as though it did
here. You were tapping exactly what produced your excruciating need for independence and the need to shatter the
taboo. You were tapping what has compelled you to live out
the imaginative life. I suspect that what comes somewhat
closer to being an autobiography of *those* impulses was the
fable, *Portnoy's Complaint*.

Where's the anger? You suggest that the anger only developed *after* Josie, a result of her insanely destructive pos-
sessiveness and then the punishment handed out to you in
court. But I doubt that Josie would have come into your life
at all had the anger not been there already. I could be wrong,
but you've got to prove it, to convince me that early on you
didn't find something insipid about the Jewish experience as
you knew it, insipid about the middle class as you experienced
it, insipid about marriage and domesticity, insipid even about
love—certainly you must have come to feel that Gayle Milman
was insipid or you would never have forsaken that pleasure
dome.

And where's the hubris, by the way? What's not here is
what it felt like to meet you—you say why, sociologically,
Josie might have fallen in love with you, but you don't say
what she might have found appealing about you. It seems to
me you relished the way you were and what you did, yet you
talk in this veiled way, or not at all, about your qualities: "the
exuberant side of my personality. . . ." How restrained and
cool. How tremendously unexuberant. Positively British. You
speak of yourself as a "good catch," but why not be more
boastful in your autobiography? Why shouldn't autobiography
be egotistical? You talk about what you were up against, what
you wanted, what was happening to you, but you rarely say
what you were like. You can't or you won't talk about yourself
as yourself, other than in this decorous way. When you give

the details of how you responded to the news of Josie's death, you don't cover anything up to make yourself look good. Yet it seems to me you're too proper to say why these women were drawn to you; at least you act that way here. But obviously it's just as impossible to be proper and modest and well behaved and be a revealing autobiographer as it is to be all that and a good novelist. Very strange that you don't grasp this. Or maybe you do but, because of a gigantic split between how you're sincere as yourself and how you're sincere as an artist, you can't enact it, and so we get this fictional autobiographical projection of a *partial* you. Even if it's no more than one percent that you've edited out, that's the one percent that counts—the one percent that's saved for your imagination and that changes everything. But this isn't unusual, really. With autobiography there's always another text, a countertext, if you will, to the one presented. It's probably the most manipulative of all literary forms.

To move on—when you're young, energetic, intelligent, you have of course to deny in yourself what you see as being part of the tribe. You rebel against the tribal and look for the individual, for your own voice as against the stereotypical voice of the tribe or the tribe's stereotype of itself. You have to establish yourself against your predecessor, and doing so can well involve what they like to call self-hatred. I happen to think that—all those protestations notwithstanding—your self-hatred was real and a positive force in its very destructiveness. Since to build something new often requires that something else be destroyed, self-hatred is *valuable* for a young person. What should he or she have instead—self-approval, self-satisfaction, self-praise? It's not so bad to hate the norms that keep a society from moving on, especially when those norms are dictated by fear as much as by anything else and especially when that fear is of the enemy forces or the overwhelming majority. But you seem now to be so strongly motivated by a need for reconciliation with the tribe that you aren't even willing to acknowledge how disapproving of its platitudinous demands you were back then, however ineluctably Jewish you may also have felt. The prodigal son who once upset the tribal balance—and perhaps even invigorated the tribe's health—may well, in his old age, have a sentimental urge to go back home, but isn't this a bit premature in you, aren't you really too young yet to have it so fully developed? Personally I tend to trust the novella *Goodbye, Columbus*, written when you were still in your early twenties, as a guide to your evaluation of the Milmans more than I trust what you care to remember about them now. The truth you told about all this long ago you now want to tell in a different way. At fifty-five, with your mother dead and your father heading for ninety, you are evidently in a mood to idealize the confining society that long ago ceased impinging on your spirit and to sentimentalize people who by now inhabit either New Jersey cemeteries or Florida retirement communities and are hardly a source of disappointment to you, let alone a target for the derisive comedy unleashed first on poor Barbara Roemer and the *Bucknellian*.

At fifty-five you may even find it hard to remember the extent of your adolescent despair over the way these people spoke and what they spoke about, over what they thought and thought about, over how they lived and genuinely expected their offspring, like you and Gayle, to live. At fifty-five, after all the books and the battles, after more than three decades of uprooting and remaking your life and your work, you've begun to make where you came from look like a serene, desirable, pastoral haven, a home that was a cinch to master, when, I suspect, it was more like a detention house you were tunneling out of practically from the day you could pronounce your favorite word of all, "away."

And if I'm right, at the end of the tunnel, waiting like your moll in the getaway car, was Josie, embodying everything the Jewish haven was not, including the possibilities for treachery—those too must have had their allure. My uneasiness is that you present yourself not as an ingenious escapee on the run from home but as little more than a victim. Here I am, this innocent Jewish boy and American patriot, my mother's papoose and Miss Martin's favorite, brought up in these innocent landscapes, with all these well-meaning, innocent people, and I fall headlong into this trap. As though you still have no sense of how you were conspiring to make it all come about.

Now, it may well be that naked in autobiography, deprived of the sense of impregnability that narrative invention seems to confer on your self-revealing instincts, you can't easily fathom your part in all this; nonetheless, after college, you simply do not present yourself as in any way responsible for what is happening. Enter Josie and, as you see it, the thing was a Pandora's box—you opened it up and everything flew out. But what makes me resist that idea is your *pursuit* of the woman. The initial flirtation is very charming and could just about have been enough, but you persist. You don't turn away from her any more than you refuse to go speak at Yeshiva, knowing when you accept that you can expect some sort of humiliating battle and, I contend, *needing* that battle, that attack, that kick, needing that *wound*, your source of invigorating anger, the energizer for the defiance. They boo you, they whistle, they stamp their feet—you hate it but you thrive on it. Because the things that wear you down are the things that nurture you and your talent.

You were passive with Josie only insomuch as you couldn't control her; otherwise, the whole thing can be seen in an entirely different way from how it reads here. You, in fact, can be seen as the real troublemaker, setting before her so tantalizingly your mother's hot tomato soup. You can also be seen, paradoxically, as the relentless aggressor practically begging Josie to behave as she did by ignoring the implications of her broken background. As you suggest, even the brightest can be awfully naïve, but anybody with tentacles and antennae would have had to know that Josie meant disaster, not after the first conversation necessarily, but surely after the first three or four weeks; certainly from the way you depict her here, only a dimwit, which you were not, would have failed to recognize the destructiveness. A good case can be made that you were deliberately drawing out of her every drop of her chaos. At the least, there is more ambiguity in your role than you are willing to acknowledge. But speaking as yourself, unprotected by the cunning playfulness of fictional masquerade, without all the exigencies of a full-scale, freewheeling narrative to overwhelm the human, if artistically fatal, concern for one's vulnerable self, you are incapable of admitting that you were more responsible for what befell you than you wish to recall.

If you want to reminisce productively, maybe what you should be writing, instead of autobiography, are thirty thousand words from Josie's point of view. *My Life as a Woman*. *My Life as a Woman with That Man*. But I hear the objection already. "Her point of view? Don't you understand, she didn't *have* a point of view—she was a bloodsucking monster. What she had were fangs!" Yes, you see her as a bitch and you can't help it and you'll never be able to help it, certainly not while speaking in your own behalf. I submit to you that she could be seen differently, and not as Lucy Nelson married to Roy Bassart in *When She Was Good*, but as herself married to the real adversary you were.

As you justly point out, she's what they now categorize and call an a.c.o.a., the adult child of an alcoholic, the victim of a victim, and therefore she has the primary trait of someone with that internal misery, the need to blame her misery on whatever external thing can be blamed. You are the child of an alcoholic father, you first blame the father. Then you marry and you blame the husband. Very likely you marry an alcoholic, unless you're an alcoholic yourself, which I happen to believe Josie was. I think she was more of an alcoholic than she was a schizophrenic. Did that never occur to you? You say that after you left her in Princeton, she'd phone you at night in New York and drunkenly charge that you were sleeping with a Negress. So she was certainly drinking then—and perhaps the progression had been slow. You say that midway through a botched suicide attempt she was "drunk and drugged." When you were living with her you probably drank wine before and at dinner—do you remember how much wine she drank? For all of your concentration on your life's predicaments, you appear to have paid remarkably little attention to a lot she did, though, to be fair, what could you, coming from your background, know about alcoholism? When it's very bad, alcoholics exaggerate any negative trait of their unfortunate partners—blow it all up and throw it at them. Very destructive stuff; *self*-destructive destructive stuff. That urine trick, which from your point of view still seems pretty wicked, didn't seem all that wicked from hers, you know. Not only do people lie when they've been drinking, but the distinction between fiction and reality is not always all that clear to them. Whatever is even faintly plausible can also seem quite real. She strongly believed that she *was* the editor of your first published stories, to her that was no lie. And she *could* have been pregnant, she thought. And you *should* have married her, she thought. And even though you didn't want to marry her, she *needed* you to marry her. And so she pulled that trick, your little Pearl Harbor. Even the obsessive jealousy, her imagining that you would do something with her little girl, that strikes me as part of the picture too.

Yes, I'm convinced that she was an alcoholic, that her disorder was hereditary, biochemical, inherited from her father, and that you didn't know it because, one, you had no idea what a *shicker* was and, two, she was young then, she ate, and she was healthy, and so the progression was not rapid. Besides, you wanted to look at her through Dostoevskian eyes then and not as though she were merely a candidate for A.A. Eventually she destroyed herself, of course—an addict like her always loses, the addict's worst fear always comes true— but all the while she continued to believe she could be good but only when *they* were good. I would even imagine that she *wanted* to be good. If only you loved her. If only the children were living with her. If only her father had been better, if only you were better, if only something external changed, she could be good again!

I said before that you were conspiring to make her happen to you, that Josie was the moll in the getaway car, but that doesn't mean I want to deny entirely that you were a victim as well—the victim of the victim of a victim. You caught the disease, as I see it, because when you live long enough with a disease you get it too. Before marrying Josie you were not that openly angry. But now you became an openly angry angry man. You became so distressingly angry that you needed psychotherapy. You owe that great explosion of anger to her. You thus owe *Portnoy* to her rather more than to Lyndon Johnson.

Am I inventing? I share the tic with you—but then my fiction, if it is fiction, is still perhaps less of a fiction than yours. Look, anything is better than My Ex-Wife the Bitch— I just cannot read that stuff. I certainly don't mean, by suggesting that she was an alcoholic, to further demean her in the human scale; nor am I saying that by not taking into account that she was an alcoholic, you may have travestied, and done an injustice to, this woman. I'm only saying that maybe it's time, twenty years on, to find another way to see her. There's still a tremendous amount of saved-up rage in that stuff about Josie, lots of microbes that are still very active. Sometimes there is a cool gap between you as you were writing this book and you as you were when these things happened, and sometimes there isn't. I felt all the way through that the book is very equivocal about that: sometimes you seem to be looking back at this twenty-four-year-old, or whatever, a little wryly and at the expense of that person, and sometimes you're looking back at this person and feeling more or less the same things. But then maybe that's how everybody looks back at his or her life and is perfectly okay.

Anyway, can *everything* about Josie have been vengeful? I suspect that Josie was both worse and better as a human being than what you've portrayed here. There were obviously times, particularly in the beginning—and you hint at this yourself—that you enjoyed her and found her appealing, and there were probably times when she was so luridly psychopathic that you still can't find your way to a proper description of the disaster you were dragged into. To be sure, I know you try hard to be generous at the conclusion of your horror story by crediting her with being your teacher in extremist fiction. But I think that's just you being astonishing—you say it to be interesting, not because you believe it. I'm telling you it also happens to be true. I tie the first period of creativity to leaving home as Joe College, and the second I tie to Josie. Everything you are today you owe to an alcoholic shiksa. Tell them *that* next time you're at Yeshiva. You won't get out alive.

Last—and then, unlike you, I'll be done with her—I think you must give Josie her real name. There's no legal reason to prevent you from using her name, and I think you owe her that. You owe it to her as a character; you owe it to her not because it would be a nice thing to do but because it's the narratively strong thing to do.

Call the other women whatever you like. (I'm assuming that all the women's names are changed—why should I not? Your changing them is only an indication of something that the book takes up, which is the conflict about whether you are a nice fellow or not.) What you call them doesn't matter, they're unimportant, they're interchangeable: they're helpmeets and sexpots and partners and pals. Actually, what's happened with these women is that not only do you disguise their identities but you shield them from your ability to see through them. You do it here and probably you do it in life, or try to. With them you pull a lot of punches (and pulling punches must finally infuriate you, as it does most everyone). With Josie, however, there are no punches pulled. The reason it's right to give Josie her real name is because she comes so close, in an elemental way, to being a peer. Josie was about who *she* was, the others are somehow about you. Josie is the real antagonist, the true counterself, and shouldn't be relegated like the other women to a kind of allegorical role. She's as real as you are—however much about yourself you may be withholding—and nobody else in this book is. You give your parents their real names, you give your brother his—and, I assume, your childhood and college friends theirs—and you say absolutely nothing about those people. So be it—it's with Josie, anyway, that you fought the primitive battle that either you didn't ever fight with your family, or you're unwilling to fight in remembering them now, or you have fought with them only by proxy, through Alexander Portnoy and through me.

I'm speaking of the primitive battle over who is going to survive. It's clear with the other women that you are going to survive. The others call forth your maturity, challenge and coerce it, and you deliver, you meet that challenge easily. With Josie, however, you regress, shamelessly and dangerously. She undoes you where ordinarily you do up everyone else. You take them up and you do them up and when you've done them up you leave them. But she undoes you and undoes you and undoes you. She even tries, driving out of Rome in that little Renault, to kill you. And then she dies. Josie's project is to incarnate destructive force and destroy the forces that try to destroy her. She is the heroine of this book, not in any sympathetic way, but that's neither here nor there when it comes to heroes and heroines. Josie is the heroine you were looking for. She provided your incredible opportunity, really—your escape from being the dominating consciousness in every situation. She took you in; she conned you. You were had. Somebody who is mentally very tricky, who hears the reverberations of everything he's ever said, somebody hypersensitively aware of his impact and very skillful at gauging it, was no longer calling the shots. She was. Honor with her name the demon who did that, the psychopath through whose agency you achieved the freedom from being a pleasing, analytic, lovingly manipulative good boy who would never have been much of a writer. Reward with her real name the destructive force that, right along with the angry Jews, hurled you, howling, into a struggle with repression and inhibition and humiliation and fear. Fanatical security, fanatical insecurity—this dramatic duality that you see embodied in the Jews, Josie unearthed in her Jew and beautifully exploited. And with you, as with the other Jews, that is not merely where the drama is rooted, that's where the madness begins.

It's only right that she have her real name in there, just as you have yours.

I don't like the way you treat May either. I don't mean the way you treat her in life; I don't care about that. I mean the way she's treated as a subject here. Here you lose your head completely—here the poor plebeian Jew from Newark is so impressed: how calm she was, how patrician she looked, how the very lines of her body bespoke guilelessness, nay, *integrity*, how very upper class her East Side apartment was. "May's uptown apartment was large and comfortably furnished without being at all this or that. Reflected the traditional tastes of her class . . ." The *awful* tastes of her class. There is nothing *worse* than the taste of the American WASP upper class. Refined? I imagine you may even have had a far more refined background than May Aldridge did. Economically pinched perhaps, uneducated, profoundly conventional, but there was a dignity, certainly, to your mother; and even when the Boss comes to the house, and the whole family is in awe of him, there is still dignity there in your father. Untutored, deprived of high culture, but *not* unrefined. I'll bet May's background was completely deprived of high culture. Her family certainly never read any real books; they went to the right schools perhaps but sure as hell didn't read the right books or give a crap about them. But you won't see that here, will you, you are so impressed. And naturally at the time you *were* impressed—but as much as this?

I don't believe it. As a reader of *Portnoy's Complaint*, of *My Life as a Man*, as a reader of what you say here about Metropolitan Life discriminating against their Jewish employees back in your father's era, I suspect a lot about her class and her background and her taste, far from impressing you, positively disgusted you. I'd bet that, as your father's avenger, you even berated her sometimes when she displayed the habits of her class and her background. But about that, nothing. Be candid—what *didn't* you like about May? There must have been plenty if you left her; I don't believe it could have been only your youthful liberty you were looking for—you also wanted to be rid of her for a very good and specific reason. So, what was it? After an emotional breakdown she dropped out of Smith and went home to Cleveland. Was there no aftereffect, no legacy of brokenness that you couldn't stand? Was she beautifully composed or utterly repressed, or were the two impossible to separate in her? Her "gentle" nature was probably as infuriating to you—because of all it implied about her vulnerability and defenselessness—as it was comforting, at first, after Josie's rages. It is chivalrous to find in yourself the sole reason for ending the affair, but in autobiography chivalry is an evasion and a lie. Maybe you are still a little in love with her or like to think that you are. Maybe at fifty-five you are suddenly in love now with those years of your life. But her idealization did not occur at the time, did it? Her idealization is a necessity of this autobiography.

You didn't want another broken woman. *That's* the reason. Of course she didn't have Josie's working-class harshness; May was placid, she stuffed her feelings, kept up her facade. But tell me, please, what was *her* addiction? Was she a pill popper like Susan McCall, her obvious embodiment in *My Life as a Man*? Surely Susan's pill popping is meant to stand for some addiction, if it isn't simply the flat-out truth. The main fear of every addict is a fear of losing, a fear of change; addicts are always looking for someone to be dependent on, they *have* to be dependent, and you were perfect. You were, after all, brought up to be reliable, and this reliability is a magnet to the broken, whether addicted, fatherless, or both. They latch on and they won't let go, and because you *are* reliable it's not easy for you to leave a job half done, especially when the reliability is being tested—and Josie went in for extreme testing, so extreme she eventually made you marry her. You're a crutch, you are flattered to be a crutch, you rush in to hold them up, and then you're holding them up and holding them up and you begin to ask yourself, "Is a crutch what I want to be?" I remember now that marathon struggle in *My Life as a Man* to make Susan come. Anything here about anything like that? Of course not. Here you investigate virtually nothing of a serious sexual nature and, somewhat astonishingly, seem almost to indicate that sex has never really compelled you.

(Polly, by the way—was she an addict too? Those martinis you talk about. But perhaps I'm overreaching to make the point, to find the pattern. You seem to paint an accurate picture of her, actually—the sweet girl out of the first romance. Another fatherless daughter, however. The only one *without* an addiction and *with* a strongly present and powerful father was Gayle Milman, our Jewish girl from suburban New Jersey. She was the most highly sexed and went on, as you say, to have an adventurous, defiant, confident career as the most desirable expatriate in all of Europe. *She* wouldn't have needed you as a crutch. Never. She needed you as a cock. So you dumped her for addicted Josie. Explain *that*.)

Even if I'm wrong and May was nothing like I suggest, you yourself don't begin to give a proper portrait of her. You don't appear to have the heart—the gall, the guts—to do in autobiography what you consider absolutely essential in a novel. You won't even say here, as you might so easily, in a footnote or just in passing, "I find it inhibiting to write about May. Even though her name has been changed, she's still alive and I don't want to hurt her, and so her portrait will have an idealized cast to it. It is not a false portrait but it is only half a portrait." Even that is beyond you, if it has even occurred to you. She is so vulnerable, this May, that even saying that might wound her horribly. But what is it you respond to in these wounded women you struggle in vain to restore to

health? That they're too helpless to dare turn you away? Yet
why would that be so with the kind of loving mother you
describe here? Unless you are idealizing your mother too, and
there we have another half portrait of another half person.
(Unless you have falsified *everyone*!) Maybe in taking care of
these women you are taking care of yourself, convalescing
from your battles, and the reason you start backing away in
the end, as you did with May, is because you're backing away
from the convalescence, because you are for the time being
feeling recovered. Maybe what you are attracted to more than
the dependency is the extremeness of these women, the intensity of their condition. I repeat: *the things that wear you
down are also the things that nurture your talent*. Yes, there
is mystery upon mystery to be uncovered once you abandon
the disguises of autobiography and hand the facts over for
imagination to work on. And no, the distortion called fidelity
is *not* your métier—you are simply too real to outface full
disclosure. It's through *dis*simulation that you find your freedom from the falsifying requisites of "candor."

Nor do you happen to fool me by suddenly bringing in a
ringer to corroborate your "facts": Fred Rosenberg writes this,
Mildred Martin has recorded that, Charlotte Maurer remembers the following, the article "Portnoy as Poppa" furnishes
confirmation of such-and-such—as though a few handpicked
witnesses to virtually nothing will make us believe everything
else.

I'm not saying that this is a conventional, self-congratulatory
celebrity autobiography. I'm not saying that the primitive,
prehistorical scene of you sitting near the site of Josie's violent
death, a happy widower being warmed by the sun, is what
you ordinarily get in people's autobiographies. But nonetheless this is still, by and large, what you get if you get Roth
without Zuckerman—this is what you get in practically *any*

artist without his imagination. Your medium for the really
merciless self-evisceration, your medium for genuine self-
confrontation, is me.

But you know as much, and nearly say as much, in a sentence near the end of your letter. "This isn't to say," you
explain, "that I didn't have to resist the impulse to dramatize
untruthfully what was insufficiently dramatic, to complicate
the essentially simple, to charge with implication what implied
very little—the temptation to abandon the facts when those
facts were not as compelling as others I might imagine if I
could somehow steel myself to overcome fiction-fatigue."

Well, you resisted the tempting impulse, all right, but to
what end? Whether the task was worth the effort is something
you had better consider thoroughly before submitting the
book for publication. By the way, if I were you (not impossible), I would have asked myself this as well: if I could admit
into autobiography that part of me—and of Polly and May,
and of Momma and Poppa and Sandy—that I can admit into
a Zuckerman novel; if I could admit into autobiography the
inadmissible; if the truly shaming facts can ever be fully borne,
let alone perceived, without the panacea of imagination. Ergo
mythology and dream life, ergo Greek drama and modern
fiction.

I will leave you with the comments—and late-night concerns—of another reader, my wife. All evening she has sat,
engrossed in your manuscript, across from the desk where I
am writing to you. As you know better than anyone, Maria
Freshfield Zuckerman is a child of the English landless gentry,
country-reared, Oxford-educated, a good-looking dark-haired
woman of twenty-eight, nearly my height, seventeen years
my junior, and the embodiment of a cultural background
markedly different from yours and mine. She has a daughter
from her previous marriage, Phoebe, a sweet and placid four-

year-old, and she is nearing the end of the eighth month of pregnancy with our first child. Maria remains very much the dutiful daughter of a well-born mother living in a Gloucestershire village, a woman without a trace of philo-Semitism, even if she has managed so far to be scrupulously tactful with me. Mrs. Freshfield's distaste for Jews generally—about which Maria's envious, unstable older sister, Sarah, had made a point of being *utterly* tactless—was the cause of a nearly disastrous misunderstanding between Maria and me earlier in my stay here. Since then I have made up my mind to ignore her mother's bias and her sister's resentment so long as neither indulges herself in my presence. If, among her neighbors in the charming village of Chadleigh, Mrs. Freshfield bemoans my "Mediterranean" looks—her response to my photograph some months before the wedding—that I view as no concern of mine.

As for my beard, its purpose is not, as Maria contends it is, to make me even more unmistakably Semitic than I already am. To begin with, when I gave up shaving three months back, I had no idea that a rabbinical appearance would be the result. If anything, the seemingly inconsequential decision to live for a while as a bearded man would seem to have to do with the fact that at forty-five I am finally on the brink of becoming a father. Marrying for the fourth time, abandoning my New York apartment and buying for the long term (and substantially reconstructing) this large London house backing onto the Thames, settling down as an expatriate in the middle of Maria's very English life—it's all this, I believe, that moved me to mark myself symbolically as a middle-aged man in the grip of a great transformation.

Nonetheless, this morning when I emerged from the bathroom still unshaven, Maria said to me, "You just won't let that die away." "What die away?" "Zuckerman amid the alien corn." "But it's quite dead as far as I'm concerned." "How can you pretend to believe that from behind that grisly thing? You will be provocative, won't you?" "I have no intention of jeopardizing my wonderful new life by provoking anyone. On the other hand, if to bestir the natives requires no more of me than a bearded face . . ." "The natives couldn't care less. It's you bestirring yourself that frightens me. It wouldn't be helpful to live through that again." I assured her that we won't. "It's an innocuous adornment," I said, "and means nothing."

And that was that, I thought, until the arrival of your manuscript, which I read through twice during the day and which Maria finished only an hour and a half ago. Since then she's been alone in bed, quite beside herself. And, mind you, at dinner her only worry had been the haircut she'd had this afternoon. "He's always cutting the wrong bits," she told me— "what is this bit doing so short, for instance?" I suggested she change hairdressers, but she is an appealingly rational, unillusioned pragmatist, admirably pliant and uncomplaining, and she replied, "Well, he does all right two times out of three." She was slightly more unnerved by our having hired a new nanny last week. With a new nanny, she tells me, you always have a lurking fear that she may be a psychopath, that she just loves torturing children. "I've cheered her up by promising her a new clothes dryer," Maria said. "You have to do that, you know—nannies have to have new clothes dryers and holidays abroad, otherwise they think they're with the wrong family." That was the extent of her apprehension, nearly all of which was feigned. She is a tremendously cooperative woman, tactfully, strategically moderate, and in a crisis reasonable and splendid. It was, as usual, a very pleasant dinner.

Then she read your book, looking up at least fifteen times to tell me what she made of it. I trust the matter-of-fact measure she takes of books; it resembles the way she sizes up people. A sample of her commentary follows, culminating in those distress-laden words that she spoke before rushing off to the bedroom, leaving me to put before you our plea.

1. She located *the* problem (for her) immediately. "Uh-oh," she said, only minutes into the book, "still on that Jewish stuff, isn't he? Doesn't bode well, does it?" "For us? Doesn't mean anything either way," I told her. She didn't look convinced but said no more. Maria does not repeat herself; that I do she'd pointed out to me when we first met. "Why," she asked, "do you have to say everything twice?" "Do I?" "Yes. When you want someone to do something, you say everything twice. Obviously you are used to being disobeyed." "Well," I said, "even *my* life hasn't been entirely without struggle." "Well, I hardly say things even once." "I wonder if it has to do," I said, "with the different ways we originated." "Those different ways," she said, "are sometimes all you can think about . . ."

2. "Always going back to his childhood," she said of you; then of herself, "I've had enough of my childhood, thanks. No more."

3. An hour passed before she looked up again. "Surely," she said, "there must come a point where even *he* is bored with his own life's story."

4. I was typing away—a draft of this letter—when I realized she was watching me very closely. Half your manuscript was by then in her lap and the other half spread around on the floor by her chair. "What is it?" I asked. "Well, I don't see why you writers shouldn't be narcissistic," she said; "it seems to me one of the flaws of character that people bring to their jobs." "We also have that obsessionality," I said. "Yes," she replied, "that's where the real trouble begins." She's thinking about my beard, I thought obsessionally.

5. Maria on your nemesis and archenemy. "It doesn't sur-

prise me at all that at twenty-five he couldn't stand up to this person who, in animal terms, had so much more fire in her belly. It doesn't seem strange in any way that he didn't know how to fight that. People who are civilized are always getting talked into being ways they don't mean to be by people who are not civilized. People are awfully weak. I know it's a convenient piece of analytic verbiage that you don't do things without wanting to. But it discounts the fact that people are also weak and at some point they just acquiesce. I'm afraid I'm an authority on this. He may not like to admit it here, but I think that's all that that marriage came down to—his weakness."

6. "Odd. As he construes it, the whole thing is a struggle against all those forces inviting him to lose his freedom. Keeping his freedom, giving it away, getting it back—only an American could see the fate of his freedom as the recurring theme of his life."

7. On randomness. "Nothing is random. Nothing that happens to him has no point. Nothing that he says happens to him in his life does not get turned into something that is useful to him. Things that appear to have been pointlessly destructive and poisoning, things that look at the time to have been wasteful and appalling and spoiling, are the things that turn out to be, say, the writing of *Portnoy's Complaint*. As each person comes into his life, you begin to think, 'So what is this person's usefulness going to be? What is this person going to provide him in the way of a book?' Well, maybe this is the difference between a writer's life and an ordinary life." "Only the subject," I said, "*is* his formative experiences as a writer. Randomness is not the subject—that's *Ulysses*." "Yes, the facts, as far as he's concerned as a writer, have to do with who he is as a writer. But there are lots and lots of other facts, all the stuff that spins around and is not coherent or *important*.

This is just such an extraordinarily, relentlessly coherent narrative, that's all. And the person who is most incoherent, Josie, has to have her incoherence made into a shape by him. All I'm saying, I suppose, is that I'm interested in the things an autobiographer like him doesn't put into his autobiography. The stuff people take for granted. Like how much you have to live on and what you eat, what your window looks out on and where you go for walks. Maybe there should, at least, be some of what Cicero calls *occupatio*. You know, 'I'm not going to talk about this, so I can talk about that,' and in that way you do talk about this." "What's it called?" I asked her. "*Occupatio*. It's one of those Latin rhetorical figures. 'Let us not speak of the wealth of the Roman Empire, let us not speak of the majesty of the invading troops, et cetera,' and by not speaking about it you're speaking about it. A rhetorical device whereby you mention something by saying you're not going to mention it. All I'm wondering is, hasn't anything *ever* happened to him that he couldn't make sense of? Because ninety-nine percent of the things that happen to me *I* can't make sense of. But maybe that's because I haven't written it all down and don't have always to be bringing *mind* to bear upon it, to go around asking myself every day, 'Well, what does this signify?' He's making everything *signify* something, when in life I don't believe it does. Mind is simply not the element in life that it appears to be here, not in mine certainly and I'd bet not in his either. I don't mean that he's presenting a deceptive image to make himself look terrific, because on the whole, for me, it's rather the other way. He looks to me awfully narrow and driven and, my God, so pleasureless. He's certainly not interested in happiness, that's pretty clear. I'd think that if something *doesn't* make great sense in his overall pattern of things, he's either bored out of his skull or terrified. He looks to me a little like what you used to look like." "Before being introduced to English randomness." "Yes," she said, "to the fact that everything isn't here to be understood and to be used but is also here because, surprisingly enough, it's life. Existence isn't always crying out for the intervention of the novelist. Sometimes it's crying out to be lived."

8. Lastly, what you elicited about men and women. "I sometimes think that men have a root neurosis about women," Maria told me. "It's really a sort of suspicion, I wouldn't lay any money on it, but I think that—forgive the childish nature of this remark—but through reading all kinds of books and through experience, I do feel that men are a bit afraid of women. And that's why they behave as they do. There are plenty of individuals who are not afraid of individual women, of course, and maybe plenty who are not afraid of women generally. But my experience has been that most of them are." "Do you think," I asked her, "that women are afraid of men?" "No," she said, "not in the same way. I'm actually, as you know, afraid of *people*. But I'm not particularly afraid of men." "Well, maybe you're right," I said, "though 'afraid' puts it too strongly." "Distrustful, then," Maria said.

When she'd finished reading, I asked the question you've asked: should it be published? "If he wants it to be," she said, "why not?" "Simply because," I said, "the only person capable of commenting on his life is his imagination. Because the inhibition is just too tremendous in this form. The self-censorship that went on here is sticking out everywhere. He's not telling the truth about his personal experience. In the mask of Philip he is not capable of doing it. In the mask of Philip he's too nice. He's the little boy nuzzling mama's seal-skin coat. It's no wonder he begins with that." "As a novelist's wife who may yet end up as her husband's subject, I'm not someone who considers niceness on a par with Nazism." "But it's surface mining," I said, "and not much more: in spite of his being very much in control of his defensiveness, the book is fundamentally defensive. Just as having this letter at the end is a self-defensive trick to have it both ways. I'm not even sure any longer which of us he's set up as the straw man. I thought first it was him in his letter to me—now it feels like me in my letter to him. It's irrelevant to say I don't trust him when the maneuvering is the message, I know, but I don't. Sure, he talks so freely about all his soft spots, but only after choosing awfully carefully which soft spots to talk about." "Well, take heart," said Maria, "maybe he'll begin doing the same for you." "No, what's motivating his selectivity is strictly self-interest. No, neither his discretion nor his shame enters into his depiction of *me*. There he is *truly* free. And where you *and* I are concerned, he's not likely ever to be as gentle and taciturn as he is about May and himself. *That* romance of anthropological contradictions is practically painless, or so he says. Where's May's anti-Semitic mother? If she even existed, offstage in Cleveland, bothering no one. Where's May's anti-Semitic sister? Nonexistent." "While mine," said Maria, able no longer to suppress her anxiety, "mine are virtually around the corner! Mine practically come to bed with us at night! Please, can't we keep to a theoretical discussion of literature?" "We were. I was pointing to what makes us more interesting than them." "But I don't *want* to be interesting! I want to be left alone with the things that are of no great interest at all. Bringing up a child. Not neglecting an aging parent. Staying sane. Uninteresting, unimportant, but *that's* what it's all about. I accept that one never gets any more from life than adulterated pleasure, but how much longer are we to be bedeviled by his Jewish fixation! I refuse to allow him to make that into a major problem again! I cannot jump, I *will* not jump, every time the needle moves on his fucking Jewish record! Especially as there is not an ounce of antag-

onism between you and me, especially as we get on so *well*—
except when he starts up with *that*! There were those months
after the blowup over my mother when everything seemed
to have resolved itself, just a lovely long period of quiet and
love. What do confrontations on that subject *achieve*? Who
even cares, other than him? I thought your New Year's res-
olution was to not make too much of a fuss about that sort of
thing. And then comes this beard! Oh, Nathan, do you really
think that beard is a good idea? You seem always to feel that
you have to explain what nobody is asking you to explain—
your right to be, and to be *here*. But no one *needs* that kind
of warranty from you. Those are—and don't go for me when
I say this—those are very Jewish feelings and frankly I believe
that if it weren't for him you would not have them. I don't
know—do you think it would help to see someone, sort of a
psychiatric sort of person, about this Jewish business? To have
spent all of this evening reading this book—and now I feel so
defenseless against what I just know is coming!"

And now, alone, in the dark bedroom she lies, terrified that
we shall never have the possibility of being other than what
you, with your obsessive biography, determine; that never
will it be our good fortune, or our child's, to live like those
whose authors naïvely maintain that at a certain point the
characters "take over" and do the storytelling themselves on
their own initiative. What she's saying is, "Oh, Christ, here
he goes again—he's going to fuck us up!"

Is Maria right? What *is* coming? Why, in her England, *have*
I been given this close-cropped, wirebrush, gray-speckled
beard? Is what began inconsequentially enough now to yield
consequences that, however ridiculous, will send us reeling
again? How can our harmonious contentment last much longer
when the household's future *is* being determined by someone
with your penchant for dramatic upheaval? How can we really

believe that this beard means nothing when you, who have rabbinically bearded me, appear in even just your first few pages to be more preoccupied than ever in your life with the gulf between gentile and Jew? Must this, my fourth marriage, be torn apart because you, in middle age, have discovered in yourself a passion to be reconciled with the tribe? Why should your relentless assessing of Jewish predicaments be *our* cross to bear!

Who are we, anyway? And why? Your autobiography doesn't tell us anything of what has happened, in your life, that has brought *us* out of you. There is an enormous silence about all that. I still realize that the subject here is how the writer came into being, but, from my point of view, it would be more interesting to know what has happened since that has ended up in your writing about me and Maria. What's the relation between this fiction and your present factuality? We just have to guess that, if we can. What am I doing exiled in this London house with a wife who wants no disturbance in her peaceful life? How much peace am I made for? Her haircuts, the nanny, the clothes dryer—how much more of that intense and orderly domesticity that I once craved can I afford to take? She is indeed making me a "beautiful" existence for the first time in my life, she is an expert in the quiet and civilized and pleasant ways of being, in the quiet and muted life, but what will that make of me and my work? Are you suggesting that without the fights, without the anger, without the conflicts and ferocity, life is incredibly boring, that there is no alternative to the fanatic obsession that can make a writer of a person except these nice dinners where you talk over candlelight and a good bottle of wine about the nanny and the haircut? Is the beard meant to represent a protest against the pallidness of all this—this randomness? Yet suppose the protest bizarrely evolves into a shattering conflict? I'll be miserable!

Well, there it is. Or there it isn't. I will let this outburst stand, absurd as I know it must be to expect even my most emotional plea to alter the imaginative course so long ago laid down for you. Similarly, I will not go back and alter what I argued earlier—that your talent for self-confrontation is best served by sticking with me—however much that argument, if persuasive to you, virtually guarantees the unfolding of the worst of our fears. Nobody who wishes to be worthy of serious consideration as a literary character can possibly expect an author to heed a cry for exceptional treatment. An implausible solution to an intractable conflict would compromise my integrity no less than yours. But surely a self-conscious author like you must question, nonetheless, whether a character struggling interminably with what appears to be the necessary drama of his existence is not, in fact, being gratuitously and cruelly victimized by the enactment, on the part of the author, of a neurotic ritual. All I can ask is that you keep this in mind when it is time for me to shave tomorrow morning.

Obligingly yours,

Zuckerman

P.S. I have said nothing about your crack-up. Of course I am distressed to hear that in the spring of 1987 what was to have been minor surgery turned into a prolonged physical ordeal that led to a depression that carried you to the edge of emotional and mental dissolution. But I readily admit that I am distressed as much for me and my future with Maria as for you. This now *too*? Having argued thoroughly against my extinction, in some eight thousand carefully chosen words, I seem only to have guaranteed myself a new round of real agony! But what's the alternative?

NEMESIS

Set in a Newark neighborhood during a terrifying polio outbreak, *Nemesis* is a wrenching examination of the forces of circumstance on our lives. Bucky Cantor is a vigorous, dutiful twenty-three-year-old playground director during the summer of 1944. A javelin thrower and weight-lifter, he is disappointed with himself because his weak eyes have excluded him from serving in the war alongside his contemporaries. As the disease begins to ravage Bucky's playground, Roth leads us through every inch of emotion such a pestilence can breed: fear, panic, anger, bewilderment, suffering, and pain. Moving between the streets of Newark and a pristine summer camp high in the Poconos, *Nemesis* tenderly and startlingly depicts Cantor's passage into personal disaster, the condition of childhood, and the painful effect that the wartime polio epidemic has on a closely-knit, family-oriented community and its children.

Fiction

THE HUMBLING

Simon Axler, one of the leading American stage actors of his generation, is now in his sixties and has lost his magic, talent, and assurance. His Falstaff and Peer Gynt and Vanya, all his great roles, "are melted into air, into thin air." When his wife leaves him, and after a stint at a mental hospital, he retires to his upstate New York country house and hopes for deliverance, which arrives in the form of the lithe, vibrant, and ever-subversive Pegeen Stapleford, the daughter of old friends and twenty-five years his junior. In this tight, surprising narrative told with Roth's inimitable urgency, bravura, and gravity, we confront the terrifying fragility of all our life's performances.

Fiction

ALSO AVAILABLE

American Pastoral
The Anatomy Lesson
The Breast
The Counterlife
Deception
The Dying Animal
Everyman
Exit Ghost
The Ghost Writer
Goodbye, Columbus
The Great American Novel
The Human Stain
I Married a Communist
Indignation
Letting Go
My Life as a Man
Operation Shylock
Our Gang
Patrimony
The Plot Against America
Portnoy's Complaint
The Prague Orgy
The Professor of Desire
Reading Myself and Others
Sabbath's Theater
Shop Talk
When She Was Good
Zuckerman Unbound

VINTAGE INTERNATIONAL
Available wherever books are sold.
www.vintagebooks.com

Printed in the United States
by Baker & Taylor Publisher Services